TREES

AND HOW TO GROW THEM.

A Guide to the

SUCCESSFUL PLANTING AND MANAGEMENT OF TREES OF EVERY KIND.

WITH ILLUSTRATIONS.

London:
WARD, LOCK AND CO.,
WARWICK HOUSE, SALISBURY SQUARE, E.C.

PUBLISHERS' PREFACE.

In the following pages the cultivation of trees has been fully treated of by an author of great practical experience. He has dealt with the subject from every point of view, and his work will be found of singular utility to all who farm plantations for the sake of a pecuniary return. We also recommend it to the notice of those who devote themselves to the planting of trees chiefly with an eye to the picturesque and beautiful.

Too little attention has hitherto been paid to the adaptation of the kind of trees that are planted to the soil and climate, and to this cause many failures are to be ascribed. The author, however, has gone carefully into this subject, and we believe has touched upon every circumstance calculated to secure success.

"Trees and How to Grow Them," we may add, forms one of our series of handbooks in which all matters relating to rural life are clearly and popularly treated, and it will certainly not be found inferior to any of its predecessors either in point of interest or in the care which has been devoted to its preparation.

CONTENTS.

LIST OF ILLUSTRATIONS.

TREES AND THEIR MANAGEMENT.

CHAPTER I.

TIMBER-TREES.

Introductory—Broad-leaved Timber-trees—The Oak—Sowing Acorns—General Mode of Cultivation—The Mossy-cupped or Turkey Oak—The Evergreen Oak—The Fulham Oak—Red, White, and Black American Oaks—The Cork Tree—The Ash—Beech—Birch—The Elm—The Hornbeam—The Locust Tree—The Plane—The Spanish Chestnut—The Maple (Sycamore)—The Sugar-Maple—Norway Maple—The Striped-Barked Maple, &c.—Broad-leaved Trees suitable for Elevated Situations—Prices of Two-year-old Trees.

1. **INTRODUCTORY.**—Perhaps, in the whole range of agricultural industry, there is no department so little understood as the planting and management of trees. Of course we except those who have made this branch their particular study, and our remarks apply to the average farmer and the amateur, who are commonly in the habit of making choice of those trees which they like best, without taking into consideration whether eithe the soil or situation is adapted for the description they have selected, and the consequence

is that great disappointment is often experienced by the tree-planter, which might have been avoided by the exercise of a little more technical knowledge.

Judicious tree-planting can be made extremely profitable, as well as causing a great improvement to the landscape; and trees can be readily found which will thrive in the most unpromising and opposite situations; so that sandy wastes can be covered with thriving plantations, as well as moist lands on the borders of streams and rivers which are subject to tidal overflow.

In the latter case they can often be made the means of forming effectual embankments against the encroachments of water, their roots in time forming a sufficient barrier to keep a stream within its proper boundary.

Of late years sea-side planting has been most successfully practised in some districts, and loose sands which used to be blown into wavy ripples by the action of the wind, upon which it was thought nothing would ever grow, are now covered with substantial plantations, which yield profit very considerable in amount to their owners.

We shall here point out, under separate divisions, the different trees most suited to every situation and soil, and the best methods of rearing each. Formerly a large proportion of our heath-lands in these islands were considered only as barren continuous tracts that would not pay for cultivation, and which would eat up so large a quantity of manure, to give even a semblance of fertility, that attempts to redeem them would be only so much money thrown away. Of late years, however, especially in Scotland, it has been demonstrated that when planted with trees, the timber which is produced on them is of a better quality and more durable nature than that grown on richer and more sheltered land; and unsuitableness of any soil can now no longer be given as an excuse for non-cultivation.

Trees of the coniferous order will thrive best on land of a light sandy texture, where scarcely any other kinds of seeds will vegetate; the broad-leaved timber-trees, as the oak, ash, Spanish chestnut and others, do best in a deep loam, in a situation not too much exposed; and in moist bog-land the willow tribes flourish and grow rapidly, as well as the alder and poplar; while trees of the American order will make the best roots in peat.

Nearly all amateurs who raise trees from seeds in quantities, for the purpose of planting-out in other situations, neglect the first element of success, which is insured by transplantation. Every kind of tree, with barely an exception or two, which we shall mention in detail, requires to be transplanted from the seed-bed at one, two, or three years of age at the utmost. The operation causes them to throw out fibrous roots which take hold of the soil, and are the means of furnishing strength and vigour to the transplanted tree.

Trees also vary considerably in their relative growth, and as fast-growing trees are often wanted for special purposes, especially where houses have been erected in bare situations, certain kinds are much more suitable than others; some of the poplar tribe attaining a height of fifty feet in twenty years, while the white and Bedford willows will quickly furnish a mass of green vegetation, and present a very decorative appearance in a very short space of time.

Other kinds, again, are more peculiarly adapted for hedge-row timber, or to form fences, from their nature being specially well fitted to afford shelter. The traveller may often see large tracts of marsh-land, intersected with deep cuttings for the purpose of drainage, into which great numbers of cattle have been turned in the summer-time, as bare as the palm of one's hand, where the poor beasts in the hot sun stand tormented by flies, without an atom of shade! Trees, in such districts, would not only afford a welcome shelter, but the loppings become a most useful addition to the produce of the farm, and a source of extra revenue.

The approaches to a house can be considerably beautified by the planting of appropriate trees, and an avenue of horse-chestnuts, which will bear transplantation at a considerable size, can speedily be created to form a striking object of adornment, which will take away that disagreeable aspect of newness which is so objectionable to the proprietor of a modern residence, which may possess in itself everything that can be desired, save that which time alone can furnish in the ordinary way. In such instances fast-growing trees can be first planted, and afterwards cut down when they can be spared, to make room for the more esteemed and slower growing orders, which may, in the mean time, be rising up to take their places.

In damp and swampy corners, where, by the natural inclination or slope of the land, water accumulates, or perhaps terminates in an unsightly pond, the weeping willow may be planted, and the situation be made beautiful by art, and an artificial lake created, surrounded by gracefully swaying branches agitated by soft breezes, and played upon by the sunshine, creating fantastic shadows, extremly pleasant to look upon.

For convenience sake we have divided our subject into separate divisions, as the planting of timber-trees, and the classification of those specially adapted to sandy and moist soils respectively; plantations or coppice (the latter being sometimes naturally grown), hedge-row timber and hedges; the formation of osier-beds; ornamental planting, &c. &c., in order to enable those who are not practically acquainted with the subject to make choice at once of any description of trees best adapted to various soils and situations.

2. **BROAD-LEAVED TIMBER-TREES.**—The principal timber-trees, which thrive best in good land moderately sheltered, are the oak, ash, elm, beech, birch, sycamore, Spanish chestnut, locust, hornbeam, walnut and plane. These do not flourish either in exposed situations, where the climate is vigorous, or in low ones surcharged with moisture, for which other species which we shall afterwards mention are exactly appropriate. An oak in an exposed and bleak situation becomes dwarfed and stunted, and is no longer "the monarch of the woods," where the Scotch pine and the cedar will attain very large proportions and assume forms of impressive grandeur.

OAK TREE.

3. **THE OAK** (*Quercus.*)—This genus is perhaps one of the most extensive we have, it being estimated that there are about one hundred and fifty species found in various parts of the world, some of diminutive, and others of very large size, about two-thirds of which number have been introduced into Britain. These, again, branch out into an enormous number of varieties, some being evergreen, some sub-evergreen, but by far the greater number consisting of deciduous trees. It will only be necessary to mention the principal varieties, the fruit of which is all alike, the whole bearing acorns (from which trees are invariably propagated), which are not usually produced until the tree attains the age of twenty years; though there are instances where they have been known to come earlier.

4. **Q. ROBUR.**—This is the best known tree of the tribe indige-

nous to Britain, comprehending many varieties, which are also found in various parts of Europe. The two most distinct are the *Q. R. pedunculata*, and *Q. R. sessiliflora*, their marked distinctiveness consisting in the former yielding its acorns on fruit stalks, while the latter produces its flowers and acorns close to the branches, without fruit stalks; the first being the variety most esteemed, as it produces the best timber, the wood of the *sessiliflora* more resembling that of Spanish chestnut. The latter, however, is more apt to

BRANCH OF THE OAK.

retain its withered leaves in the winter during its youth, its chief recommendation being that it grows more freely than the other while young, especially in inferior soils and situations, but when they have attained a certain age there is but little perceptible difference in their rates of growth.

The more common tree of the two, both of which are styled the British oak, is the *pedunculata*, which is the most frequently met with both in the natural as well as the planted woods of Great Britain.

5. **SOWING THE ACORNS.**—Beds are prepared by being well dug, and are in nurseries generally four feet wide, and twenty-five

feet long, one bushel of sound acorns being sufficient for a bed of this size.

As the future plants will depend greatly upon the quality of the seed used, acorns should be collected from the most approved trees, and those only of the largest size employed, as the smallest acorns produce plants which continue to be of a slow and feeble growth for some years. They will vegetate in any kind of soil, but that which is light and friable is best adapted for young trees. The acorns generally become ripe, and drop from the oaks about the end of autumn, and they can be sown at any time between then and the beginning of March.

Where a number of beds are laid out, the alleys between them are commonly made about fourteen inches wide, the soil from these alleys being used to cover the seed, which, in the case of heavy soils, should be at the depth of half an inch only, but in those which are light and friable the covering should be nearly an inch in depth. The acorns should be placed in position, and either rolled, or beaten down with the back of a spade.

If the operation of sowing is performed during the winter, or in early spring, the soil from the alleys should be only thrown on roughly (but taking care that the seeds are well hid) and allowed to remain in this condition until April, exposed to the influence of frosts, by which time the land will become thoroughly pulverised, when it should be raked and made smooth. The rake will destroy the weeds which have begun to vegetate, and early in May the young plants will make their appearance, being able to easily penetrate the soft surface. As the young oaks at this period are very tender and are sometimes injured by late frosts, it is desirable to give them some light covering, such as branches of evergreens, leaves, litter, or similar light substances, till the end of May, when they can be removed, and nothing more requires to be done, except to keep the beds clear of weeds.

At one year, but more frequently at two years of age, the seedling plants are transplanted into nursery lines, sixteen or eighteen inches asunder, the plants being six inches from one another in the lines. This can be done any time during winter or spring in fine open weather, taking care that the earth in the seed-bed is carefully loosened, so that the lateral fibres of the young trees are not injured in their removal. The tap-root is not of such great consequence, as it is best always to cut off its extremities. After standing in the nursery lines for two years, they will generally be found to have attained a height of from two to three feet, and are then fit to be placed out on the site of the future plantation.

If a larger size is required for planting out, they should at this age be again transplanted into a wider space, and allowed to remain there for two or three years, according to their growth and progress, when they will be fit to be used for hedge-row plants, or for similar situations where smaller ones are liable to be destroyed by the attacks of vermin. If allowed to stand more than two years without being transplanted, the tap-root of the oak strikes deeply down into the soil, and loses that bushiness which is so essential, and even indispensible, for re-planting. They may appear well-grown and vigorous, but from want of this development of fibrous roots they will be but of small value for planting.

As the roots of the oak penetrate the soil to a greater depth than almost any other tree, its future prosperity and growth depends very much upon the qualifications of the subsoil. It succeeds best on a strong, deep soil, considerably elevated above stagnant water; but oaks of large size are grown in sandy or gravelly soil when it is composed of a clayey mixture, and will do very well upon land in which ash or elm will not grow satisfactorily, and are often seen to answer in soils of different qualities. In rich, sheltered valleys, when grown with other trees, it grows with a tall trunk, and becomes a lofty tree, but in bare and exposed situations it becomes dwarfed and bushy.

When planted closely together, during the early stages of its growth the young oak is erect and pliant; but before it attains its full height, which depends much upon situation, its ramifications become more marked, its outline being very much affected by its surroundings. Its natural habit of growth can only be identified when it stands alone, and its roots are seen taking a firm hold, and insuring a solid foundation in the soil, forming a massive trunk, with ponderous horizontal branches.

The oak leaf expands at a somewhat late period in the season, and is frequently affected by the last frosts, so that in exposed situations they should be reared with faster growing trees, to act as nurses, as the spruce-fir, Scotch fir, larch, or beech, it being the general practice in Scotland, in some bleak exposures, to have firs planted a few years previously, which attain a height of about four feet before the young oaks are put in. When this shelter has been provided, the young tree rapidly establishes itself firmly in the soil, and is seldom killed by confinement, being tenacious of life. After being relieved from confinement, it regularly makes rapid progress, throwing out summer and autumn shoots, which are peculiar to this tree and a few others while young and vigorous.

Oak trees which have had shelter in their youth have been known to attain a height of upwards of seventy feet, with clean branchless trunks of more than forty feet. But these straight trunks are not always desired, as crooked ones are more valuable for some purposes, such as ship-building, than straight ones, and in order to produce them it is often customary to cut off the leading shoot, and leave two or three of the strongest lateral branches, the next strongest being shortened in order to impede their progress. This treatment generally causes the trunks to grow crooked, though in some cases the shoots left will incline to the perpendicular.

Although the oak while young does not grow so fast as many hard-wooded trees, yet after the age of twenty years it will make about equal progress with them.

One advantage in connection with the oak is that when the timber is felled a new plantation is not required, as the roots readily spring, and for the first few years will grow twice as fast as those newly planted—a very desirable feature where wood is wanted, as there is mostly a difficulty in immediately establishing a plantation where timber has been grown before.

6. **MOSSY-CUPPED OR TURKEY OAK** *(Q. cerris).*—This species is remarkable for the great number of varieties which it produces from seed, differing in the size and shape of their leaves, and being inclined to hybridise with the evergreen oak: thus a great number of sub-evergreen plants can be obtained from those raised, if a little pains is taken in their selection.

The tree was introduced into Britain in 1735, being a native of the middle and south of Europe and the west of Africa. While possessing an elegant appearance, it is as hardy as the common oak, grows faster, and will thrive in poorer soil. The leaves are of bright green above, inclining to white underneath, being lobed and sinuated. They die in autumn, but adhere to the tree throughout the winter.

It is propagated in the same way as the common oak, ripening its acorns in the like manner; but, as the young plants are taller, it is usual to remove the seedlings into nursery lines at one year, instead of allowing them to stand in the seed-bed for two years. In a good soil the tree will reach a height of forty feet in twenty years, generally growing with a straight trunk; but thirty feet may be set down as the common average height it will attain during this period. In its growth it more resembles the larch than the British oak, being deficient in those grandly spreading, massive branches which characterise the latter. Some of the oldest trees in the southern counties of the kingdom stand upwards of one hundred feet high. Its timber is beautifully veined, and takes a fine polish, but is not so durable as that of the common oak.

7. **THE EVERGREEN OAK** *(Q. ilex).*—This tree forms a very handsome evergreen, its foliage being very abundant, of a rich dark green colour, and is the well-known evergreen tree of the principal Italian cities, being a native of the south of Europe and north of Africa, although it has been cultivated in Britain from a very remote period.

The acorns ripen abundantly in England, but as the plants produced from them are found to make a principal tap-root when sown in a seed-bed, bare of fibrous roots, and difficult to remove without injury, they are generally grown in small flower-pots, one acorn being planted in each, and the young seedlings removed into larger pots, according to their growth.

This tree is well adapted for the embellishment of towns, as it stands a smoky atmosphere better than most evergreens, its foliage having a fine polish, with a downy tinge underneath its leaves. Its growth varies very considerably in different situations, which is doubtless owing to the great number of varieties of which the genus is composed. It generally attains the height of forty feet, but has been known to reach an altitude double that number when favourably placed as to soil and shelter. It is tender when young, and is of slow growth, but when once established it makes steady progress, and is a tree of great duration, blossoming in May and June, and throwing out male flowers, or catkins, from one to two inches long on the shoots of the former year, the female flowers being produced on the newly formed twigs, and the acorns coming to maturity during the second year. Its timber is heavy, tough, and strong, and when grown in sufficient space it usually forms an immense trunk, which it conceals with its foliage down to the surface of the ground. In Italy its branches are lopped, and fresh ones induced to spring up perpendicularly, with the view of forming a handsome evergreen screen, in positions where such are required. The tree is remarkably free from disease, and, it is said, will stand and retain its vigour for a thousand years.

8. **THE FULHAM OAK.**—There are a great number of hybrids, of which the above is one of the finest specimens, commonly supposed to be between the mossy-cupped and the cork tree. The acorns of the original tree have yielded many varieties, and as they "sport" very much, grafting is resorted to for the purpose of propagating the species in its purity on the common or Turkey oak, and on stocks of ordinary vigour. The grafts will frequently attain the height of three or four feet in course of the first summer.

9. **TURNER'S EVERGREEN OAK.**—This is a hybrid between the common British and evergreen oak, resembling in summer time the appearance of the former; but in autumn its foliage assumes a more massive appearance, being dark green and glossy. Like other hybrids, it is propagated by grafts, and will grow as quickly as the common oak till it attains the age of twenty years. It is a capital evergreen, as its healthy specimens retain the leaves of the former year throughout the summer. Unlike the Fulham oak, this variety has not been known to bear acorns.

10. **WHITE, BLACK, AND RED AMERICAN OAKS.**—Some of the latter are extremely ornamental, particularly the *Q. coccinea*, or scarlet oak, common to New Jersey, Georgia, and Pennsylvania. It grows more rapidly than the common oak, and was introduced into

Britain about the end of the seventeenth century. Although it produces acorns in this country, the trees are generally propagated by imported seed, which require to be sown immediately after their arrival. They are treated in the same way as ordinary oaks, but having the same tendency as the *Q. ilex* to form a bare tap-root, which produces a stunted plant when transplanted, they require to be moved early into nursery lines before the roots get strong.

The leaves of the tree are deeply sinuated, of a bright, shining green, which not only vary considerably on different trees, but on the same tree at separate stages of its growth. The first frost of winter changes them to a bright yellow or red, which ultimately merges into the most vivid crimson or scarlet. They are deciduous, and produced on long leaf stalks, some of the specimens being a foot long and six inches broad on luxuriously growing trees. The timber of the white, red, and black American oaks is generally soft and porous and therefore but little esteemed, but the richness of effect the trees themselves give when planted in appropriate situations causes them to be very valuable for decorative effect, as lawn or park trees, frequently assuming a broad, spreading form, having a beautiful appearance on the margin of woods and plantations.

CORK TREE.

11. **THE CORK TREE** (*Q. suber*).—This species furnishes the cork of commerce, its cultivation being the same as that of the common evergreen oak, though it is less hardy, and seldom attains a height above forty feet. It is a native of the same districts as the *Q. ilex*, abounding on dry, hilly situations. It is cultivated chiefly for the sake of its outer bark, which is the cork. When the tree is young, the trunk is stripped of its branches to the height of eight or ten feet, and when it has reached a certain age—generally from twenty to thirty years—the outer coating of its bark is found to consist of a

formation of coarse, porous cork, mixed with woody substances. This is stripped off in July or August, and in eight or ten years another cover is formed of a better quality than the first, but it is not until the third disbarking that the cork is considered to have attained its proper quality and thickness. The operation is continuously performed at the same recurring intervals, care being taken not to wound the inner bark, or wood of the tree. Strange to say, this operation produces no injurious effect upon it, but has rather a contrary effect.

The ragged, corky bark, of a whitish hue, contrasts very forcibly with the dark-green, luxuriant foliage of the tree, which, it is said, will stand for several centuries.

12. **THE ASH** (*Fraxinus excelsior*).—The ash is one of the most graceful trees we possess, and though deficient in the massive grandeur which distinguishes the oak, it takes nearly equal rank with it, and as a landscape decoration the ash is nearly perfect. The tall, or common ash flourishes best in a deep hazelly loam, near a stream on a slope inclining towards it, where, without being in absolute contact with much water, its roots may have access to it during the heats of summer.

Ash Tree.

The ash requires to be grown quickly, and differs in its nature from Scotch firs, cedars, and other trees the timber of which is considerably improved by the process of a slow growth. In the case of the ash, if checked in its progress by the natural poorness of the land, or by its roots coming in contact with a sour, wet subsoil, the wood becomes brittle, and of very inferior quality.

The growth of the ash needs to be stimulated by a good soil and somewhat sheltered situation. It flourishes well enough in elevated positions provided they are not exposed; that is to say, the ash will do well upon the slopes of steep elevations so that it has moderate shelter, and the finest specimens of the ash are often seen on the sides of the glens and ravines of hilly districts and countries.

The ash is propagated by seeds, which become ripe in November, and as they are tolerably abundant all over the country, the seeds from the best trees only should be used, which require somewhat exceptional treatment. When collected in sufficient quantity, they should be put into a pit made in a light, porous soil, and mixed up with the earth or sand in the proportion of one bushel of seed to two of earth, where they must be allowed to remain for fifteen months, the seeds and soil intimately blended together, being turned over at least half a dozen times during that period. This operation is necessary to ensure success, for if sown before, the tender plants suffer from frosts. At the end of February (a year and a quarter after they have been gathered) the seeds should be sifted, and sown in beds consisting, if possible, of good sandy loam. They thrive well in land upon which carrots have been grown that has had a fair share of manure applied to it; or will do to follow turnips and potatoes, when the land has been well manipulated. This should be thoroughly dug over again, and raked, and marked out in beds of four feet in width, with an alley one foot wide between them. With an inverted rake, half the surface of the bed is uncovered for the reception of the seed, the soil being evenly pushed off into the alley. The workman then stands in the alley immediately behind the ridge of earth pushed off, and then uncovers the other half in a similar manner, which avoids trampling on the beds. The seeds are then sown about half an inch from one another, and covered over with about three quarters of an inch of soil. The men employed in nurseries who are used to this kind of work quickly cover over the seeds with a rake, but it is better, perhaps, to use a clean spade, and spread the earth lightly over them.

After standing for two years in the seed-bed, they should be transplanted into lines a foot and a half asunder, the plants standing about six inches from one another.

After standing thus for two years longer, they will then be fit for planting-out in those situations they are destined ultimately to occupy.

As a rule, the method we have described for planting will apply to nearly all our hardy tree seeds, except in those instances where a different course of treatment is necessary, which we shall duly specify in order.

The qualities which constitute excellence in the ash are strength, toughness, and durability; and these are best secured by a free and uninterrupted growth. This is hastened by a good soil and somewhat sheltered situation, but the trees must not be crowded by others of a different kind, though it is immaterial if the branches jostle one another, as they are loose-headed and open growing, and thrive best when planted in masses by themselves.

In some cases it may be necessary for them to have nurses during the first fifteen years of their growth, but after that time their progress should not be interfered with by the near neighbourhood of other trees.

In a high situation, after the land has been well trenched, holes should be dug with the common garden spade about a yard apart, one half being for nurses, which will take about 5,000 plants to the acre. In sheltered positions five feet asunder will be sufficient, making the average to be about 500 nurses, and 1,700 ash plants.

The months of October, November, March and April are the best to plant in, and the sites for the permanent position of the ash should be carefully chosen. No tree is so soon injured by *stagnant* water, and the land should always be well drained. If this is done they succeed well enough in moist situations where the water runs off. Ash grown on loose boggy soils is not worth more than two-thirds of the value per cubic foot of that raised on hazelly loams and in other favourable situations, besides producing a much smaller quantity of timber. From carefully tested experiments made upon a large scale, of trees of the same age and quality, planted in different situations, at fifty years of age some contained only thirty cubic feet of timber, whilst others were found to have nearly eighty!

Thinning and pruning should be well attended to, and what is got in this way is often extremely valuable. As hop-poles and for many other puposes the wood is not surpassed by that of any other tree, and is most useful in the construction of many agricultural implements, as handles to rakes, shovels, spades, forks, mattocks, picks, &c., and the timber is largely used in the construction of ploughs, harrows, axle-trees, and for carriage work of all sorts.

The ash being a handsome tree of graceful appearance, may often be seen in hedge-rows throughout England. It is not at all calculated for this purpose, however, as for a large circle round about it the land is rendered perfectly unproductive, and it is not nearly so well adapted as the oak or the elm for hedge-row timber.

13. **THE BEECH** (*Fagus sylvatica*).—The beech is not only one of the handsomest, but for the purpose of shelter can be made one of the most useful trees possible in the neighbourhood of the farm or farm-buildings. In fact, there is no tree so useful in its living state as the beech, as it will grow almost anywhere in prepared soil. When young it retains its dead leaves during the winter, and where the soil is not naturally rich, and this is an object for the purpose of shelter, it should be well matured to ensure their retention.

Beech fences are to be met with upwards of thirty feet high in some parts of the country, which are found most valuable for protection of lambs in winter and spring by those who rear great numbers. It is supposed to be indigenous to Britain, and few trees have so ornamental an appearance. In "leafy June" its leaves get hard, and assume a dark, rich, shining green colour, which contrasts with the delicate silken foliage it first assumes when emerging from its firm, spiky buds. When planted on the slopes of hills where the subsoil is calcareous it will often assume the feathery appearance of the birch. Its stem is massive, the bark being of a silvery hue, and when its leaves are wetted by a summer shower they glisten in the sunshine in the most beautiful manner.

BEECH TREE.

It is propagated by its "mast," or seed, which becomes ripe in October, and the best way to obtain it is to spread a large sheet, or cloth, beneath the tree, and shake its branches violently. The bad seeds, which contain no kernel, are the first to fall, and these should be rejected. If, however, from unavoidable causes bad and good have been got together, the latter may easily be separated from those which are worthless by throwing them into a tub half full of water. The good seeds will sink to the bottom, while the worthless ones will float on the top. They should be immediately separated, and the good seed thoroughly dried, and when quite free from damp or moisture be put up in bags or boxes, mixed with twice their bulk of sand,

and put aside till the time of sowing comes round, which extends from the last fortnight in March till about the middle of April.

Some writers recommend autumn sowing, but the seeds are subject to the depredations of mice, at a time of year when the food of these vermin is not so easily procurable, and they are also likely to be frost-bitten, as autumn-sown seeds germinate in April, and thousands of young plants have been known to be cut off by the late frosts.

The mode of sowing the seed, and the after treatment of the plants, is the same as that followed in the case of the ash, with the exception that the seeds should receive a covering of an inch of soil, and the nuts lie an inch asunder, which it will be as well to affix in their positions, in the same way as acorns are done, by gently patting them down with the back of a spade.

In planting, the same distances should be assigned to them as that recommended for the ash, but the trees should be well established before they are pruned, as when the knife is used too early they frequently become bark-bound, and refuse to grow. This will also happen if plants are employed which have stood more than two years in the seed-bed without being transplanted. When this takes place, the best course is to cut them down in April nearly close to the ground—say three or four inches from it—and choose a straight shoot to form the future tree.

As the beech has a tendency to throw out spreading branches, if timber is the object of their growth they should be allowed to stand for some years somewhat close to one another, so as to discourage the growth of the side spray, and afterwards to thin them out when they have attained a sufficient altitude, and let in air and light, and the play of the elements.

The beech is not a profitable tree to grow in some soils, but will answer in most dry ones, preferring sand, light loams, and loams with chalky bottoms. On chalk beds no other tree will grow so well, except, perhaps, the walnut.

The leaves of the beech are an excellent substitute for straw or chaff in stuffing matresses. They should be collected together immediately after they fall for this purpose, and carefully dried. They will remain sweet for five or six years.

Beech-nut oil is a considerable article of commerce in France, but the climate of England does not appear to be favourable for developing the oily secretions of the nut, so as to make its extraction a successful commercial operation.

14. **THE BIRCH.**—There are two varieties of the birch, natives of Britain, *Betula alba*, and *B. a. pendula*, the latter being by far the most ornamental in appearance, and valuable.

The tree is indigenous throughout the northern countries of

Europe and on elevated situations in the south of it, and the two varieties may be readily distinguished. When a plant, ***B.a. pendula*** is found covered over with rough exudations, while the common tree is soft to the touch, and perfectly smooth. It adapts itself to many soils and situations, and only one or two other species are found growing so near to the North Pole.

The common tree is the shorter of the two, when growing wild attaining a height of about thirty feet, while the weeping variety is generally nearer forty; but when cultivated in plantations both sorts grow considerably taller, especially when blended and mixed with other trees.

BIRCH TREE.

The birch has often been admired decorating the margins of lakes and rivers, and standing in solitary glens and ravines; and though often found growing freely in wet and swampy ground, yet few trees can so well resist drought, adapting itself to the most diversified soils and situations.

In remote, hilly districts, the birch may frequently be found in coppice, on rocky hills, where scarcely any other kind of tree will grow, and it frequently springs up naturally on land where Scotch pine has been felled, the exuviæ of the pine, which is fatal to plants in general, appearing to encourage the growth of the birch.

Some of the finest weeping birches in the kingdom are to be seen in Scotland, where they are to be found sixty feet in height, with trunks six feet in circumference, throwing out pendulous masses of spray ten feet long, and forming objects of great beauty.

The seeds of the birch tree usually get ripe in September, when they are spead out thinly to dry in an airy place, and put away till the following March, which is the best time for sowing.

Beds of four feet in width should be formed in friable, sandy, peat soil, if possible, which should be smoothly dug over, leaving an alley a foot in width between each; and the seed spread evenly on the surface of the ground, at the rate of one bushel of clean seed to each bed of thirty lineal yards. It needs no covering, but in dry weather the seeds are pressed closely down into the ground with the feet; and during the early summer, if the weather turn out very dry, it is best to shade the beds with branches of spruce-fir or any other appropriate covering.

At one year old the young plants are removed from the seed-bed into lines twelve inches apart, standing three or four inches from each other in the rows. They are allowed to remain two years standing thus, when they generally get from two to three feet high, and are then fit for finally planting out. Well-grown plants at a year old are generally six inches high.

The birch is frequently used as a nurse for other trees, such as the oak, chestnut, &c., till they pass through their tender infancy, when they are removed. The brushwood is found very useful in forming wicker fences to prevent the marauding tendencies of cattle and sheep. Reaching maturity at about seventy years of age, it seldom increases in bulk after this period, though it depends very much upon the soil and situation they occupy.

As underwood, or coppice, it is usually cut every five or six years, and for bark, every eighteen or twenty years. Birch bark is held in high estimation for tanning, being amongst the most indestructible of vegetable substances, and is preferred on this account by fishermen for tanning their nets and cordage, causing them to be soft and flexible, and encouraging the elastic qualities so desirable in articles of this description.

As fuel for smoking hams and herrings, the wood of the birch is highly appreciated; while the timber takes a high polish, and, being often beautifully marked, is frequently used in veneering and for articles of furniture.

The sap of the tree is made to flow by boring a hole in the trunk in summer time, or during warm weather at the end of the spring, which is the product known as "birch-wine." To obtain this wine great numbers of trees have been destroyed by the soldiery in different parts of Europe during various campaigns.

Some of the American varieties of the birch-tree attain a greater size than those indigenous to Great Britain, many of them having larger leaves and wearing a different appearance to the tree familiar to us in England. The cherry birch of Pennsylvania (*Betula lenta*) yields beautiful timber of a large size.

15. **THE ELM** (*Ulmus*).—There are two leading species of the elm tree most commonly abundant in this country, the *U. campestris*, or English elm, and the *U. montana*, or the mountain or wych elm, both of which occupy a deservedly high place amongst British timber trees, it being the most common tree, excepting the oak,

perhaps, and few kinds making so much valuable timber in the same space of time.

There are about twenty kinds of the *U. campestris* generally cultivated, which are chiefly propagated by layers from stools, or from suckers from old trees. It is a native of the middle and south of Europe, where it yields seed abundantly, being remarkable for its

ELM TREE.

tendency to produce seedling varieties, which causes the species to be very confused.

In France immense numbers of trees are yearly raised from seed, but as it seldom produces seed in England it is questionable whether it is indigenous to our country, though it must have been introduced at a very early age, and propagated by the ordinary methods followed.

Its erect form, which furnishes a tall bole, and its clustering foliage and somewhat dense habit of growth, render it a striking object, its trunk being remarkable for the uniformity of its diameter throughout, naturally rising in a straight form, and seldom wanting pruning.

A stool is formed by topping over a plant that has become well established in the soil, when, during the ensuing summer, it will throw out a number of young shoots. When these have done growing for the season, they should be bent down into the earth, and well fixed in it at a depth of five or six inches, so

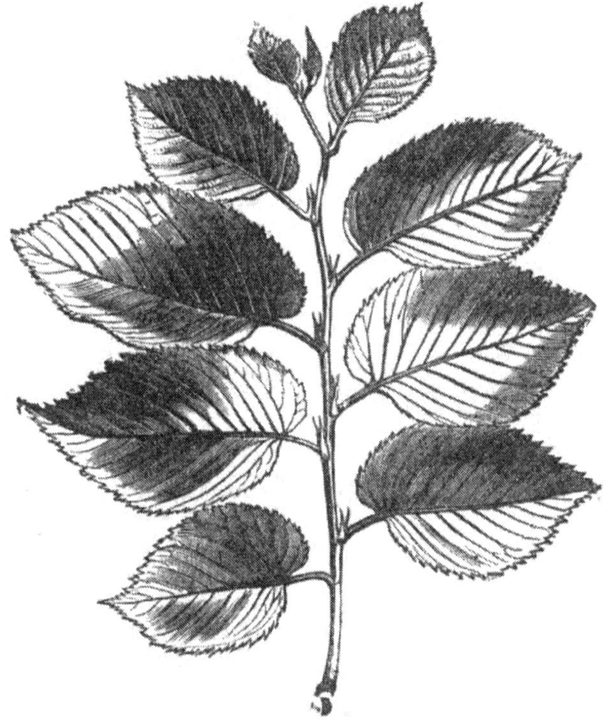

LEAVES OF ELM.

placed as to leave their extremities in an erect position above the ground. During the ensuing summer these layers become rooted, and the stool throws out another crop of shoots. The layers which have rooted should be removed, any time during winter or in early spring, so as to make room for the succeeding young shoots to be bent down in the manner which has been described, and each year a fresh crop of young plants can be raised.

The stool should stand in a rich, friable, sandy soil, when the young shoots will strike readily; and if not of a sandy nature, a few shovelsful of sand may be placed around it with advantage.

If the ground is clean and of the best quality, the young plants may be placed out at once; but if their future destination is not in soil of a rich description, they should be put into nursery lines for two years before being finally planted out, a foot apart, the lines being two feet asunder.

The elm, like the birch, may be seen growing in soils of very opposite qualities, from the driest sand to a moist clay; but a deep, rich, soft soil, with a subsoil of an open texture, is the most favourable for the best development of its growth. Its root, when young, naturally has a tendency to produce bushy fibres, which peculiarly well fits it for transplantation, even when it has attained a size beyond that usually reached by young trees destined to occupy other situations, and in a fair soil it will generally attain a height of twenty-five feet in ten years.

The elm often attains a very large size, good specimens containing as much as three hundred to four hundred and fifty cubical feet of timber, ranging from one hundred and twenty-five to one hundred and fifty feet high. It generally arrives at maturity in seventy or eighty years, after which it has a tendency to become hollow in the centre, and in high gales of wind unsound trees which have stood as prominent objects in an avenue leading to a mansion are sometimes laid low when so affected, from which even young trees are not entirely exempt.

The wood of the elm being brown, of a hard and fine grain, and not apt to crack, is valuable for many special purposes, being much used in London for coffin-making, its value being regulated by its quality, which varies a good deal. Many of the seedling varieties which have been occasionally raised from seed, spread throughout the country, are of fable growth, and possess but little value as timber-trees. This aptitude to sport has caused the genus to be somewhat confused, so that botanists are sometimes unable to determine satisfactorily which are species, and which varieties only.

16. **THE MOUNTAIN, OR WYCH ELM** (*U. montana*).—This tree does not attain the height of the tall English elm, but it is very valuable as a timber tree, though yielding a shorter bole, and being of much slower growth. It has a more spreading habit than *U. campestris*, is hardier in constitution, with bolder ramifications of branches, and is more picturesque in appearance, adorning the glens and mountain sides of Scotland, of which country it is a native.

About fifty feet is its average height, but it often reaches a higher altitude when mingled with other trees. It does not produce suckers like the English elm, but is propagated by seed, which it yields freely, and from which many varieties have of late years been raised.

The seeds get ripe usually about the middle of June, when they should be gathered, and immediately sown in beds prepared for their reception, composed of rich, friable soil, four feet broad. The seeds are often very unequal in quality, half perhaps, in some instances, out of any given quantity not possessing the power of germinating, and the quantity employed must, to a certain extent, be left to the judgment of the person saving the seed; but a bushel is generally thought sufficient for a bed of twelve lineal yards, with the object of raising plants about two inches apart.

Half an inch of soil should be spread over the seeds, and the beds should be watered and shaded in dry weather. About a week after sowing, the plants will make their appearance, when the shading may be discontinued, and no further care is necessary, except to keep the beds clear of weeds during the summer. In the following winter, or early spring, they can be removed into nursery lines, but they are frequently allowed to remain in the seed-bed for two summers when they do not stand too thickly. The nursery lines should be a foot and a half apart, and the plants stand six inches from one another. Here they should stand for two years, but if allowed to remain longer without being removed, the roots are apt to get bare, after which the plant will often become stunted when transplanted, and will not grow freely.

The tree blossoms in April just before the leaves expand, and will grow rapidly, and produce heavy timber in a deep rich soil with an open sub-soil, but where water stagnates near the surface its growth becomes feeble, and lichen will often be found overspreading its bark. It is pruned to the greatest advantage from eight to fourteen years of age, at this epoch of its existence being apt to ramify near the ground, and to form a shorter trunk than is desirable. By shortening the shoots, and curtailing some of the strongest lateral branches, a more upright growth will be encouraged than that to which the tree would naturally incline and the trunk by this means become lengthened.

17. **THE WEEPING ELM** (*U. pendula*).—This is a picturesque tree, presenting a very ornamental appearance, of which there are several varieties. It is thought to have sprung originally from the mountain elm, from its large leaves and habit of growth, which is of somewhat peculiar character. Nurserymen have paid a good deal of attention to this variety of late years; it seeds freely, and plants raised from them are apt to lose the peculiarities of the species, and in order to preserve them it is usual to graft on tops

of the common elm, which soon forms a head of striking appearance, and grows very rapidly in a very diversified fashion, its branches shooting out in all directions.

As a decorative tree for lawns, parks, or pleasure grounds, it is one of the best of the fast-growing trees, its general effect approximating somewhat to the cedar. There are also several varieties of cork-barked elm (*U. suberosa*) which are well worthy of a place amongst other trees, as well as the variegated and curled-leaf elms. Another rapid-growing species which is frequently met with in various parts of England is *U. glabra*, as well as *U. g. vegeta*, which is not only one of the fastest growing, but makes capital timber.

18. **THE HORNBEAM** (*Carpinus*).—The common hornbeam (*C. betula*) resembles somewhat in its foliage the leaves of the common beech, but without their high polish. As a timber tree it is very little cultivated in this country, but is chiefly valuable as a hedge plant. It stands pruning better than the beech, and is not subject to disease when grown for a length of time in a confined position.

THE HORNBEAM.

As a timber tree it occupies a position between the beech and the birch, often producing flat and irregular trunks which are by no means ornamental, and although large trees of this genus may be occasionally met with, it does not commonly attain a very large size. Of the three or four species comprehended in the genus, they are all deciduous, yielding unisexual flowers, the male and female being in distinct catkins on the same plant.

The tree is indigenous to England, Ireland, the south of Scotland, and many European countries, not liking either cold or hot climates, its timber being by no means valuable, though useful enough for many purposes where a white, tough wood is wanted, being at one time much used for milk vessels, yokes for cattle, and handles of tools, possessing great powers of resistance, but little flexibility.

As an agricultural plant its main value, therefore, consists in its forming such capital screen fences in windy and exposed situations;

thriving well on nearly all kinds of soil; growing quickly even on cold clay, especially when planted thickly. It is superior to the beech as a hedge plant, as it derives its support from a deeper depth in the ground, and is therefore less injurious to the neighbouring growing crops.

Growing close and "twiggy," it retains its leaves far on in the autumn, but not throughout the winter so commonly as the beech, nor does it form so compact a hedge after several years of growth though its progress is quicker during the first six or eight years of its existence. It admits of being freely pruned, and can therefore be trained in any form, and readily springs when lopped over, at any height from the surface of the ground.

The seeds are contained in a small nut, which usually ripens at the end of autumn, and are generally sown in spring, lying dormant for the first year, and vegetating in the ensuing spring. When sown in the autumn immediately after becoming ripe, they start up unequally, and a small proportion will vegetate during the first spring.

A bed of four feet in width, and fifty yards long, is generally sown with a bushel of clean seed, and covered with about half an inch of soil! If they spring up too thickly they are thinned out, and transplanted at a year old, but if they come up thinly they are allowed to stand in the seed-bed for two years, and are then placed in nursery lines about a foot and a half apart, the plants standing about six inches from one another. After standing thus for two years they are then fit for hedge plants, but if they are allowed to remain longer without being transplanted they are apt to assume a tree-like form, and become tall and bare near the surface, which causes them to be unfit for hedge plants. When this happens, however, they can be cut down close to the ground, when they will spring up again in a bush-like form.

When first lifted from the seed-bed the extremities of their roots should be cut off, in order to induce them to throw out a fibrous growth.

Of the common species, the incised leaf and the variegated are the principal varieties. Charcoal made from the wood of the hornbeam is highly esteemed in the manufacture of gunpowder, for forges, and in cooking; ranking high for throwing out a great heat, for its durability, and its brightness.

The smaller species, as *C. orientalis*, and *C. americana*, are not of a useful character, being but of small growth, and never cultivated as timber trees.

19. **THE LOCUST TREE** (*Robinia pseud-acacia*).—Also called the False Acacia. A leguminous tree. The common *Robinia* is a native of North America, a great impetus having been given to its cultivation in this country by William Cobbett, who imported a great quantity of seeds from America and raised a great number of

plants, which he sold under the name of the locust tree between the years 1820 and 1825.

Cobbett puffed it extensively in his *Woodlands* and other publications, praising it to the skies as being superior to any other tree, on account of the rapidity of its growth and the durability of its timber, which was ultimately destined to eclipse the oak in England.

Many people bought the tree thinking they were obtaining an entirely new description, and for some time it was planted to an unprecedented extent throughout the country, not being recognised as the *Robinia pseud-acacia* which had before been introduced into Europe about the year 1635.

LOCUST TREE.

Loudon describes a specimen which was planted in that year in the Jardin-des-Plantes, Paris, which two hundred years after, *i.e.* in 1835, had grown to be seventy-eight feet high, though it is usually a tree of somewhat small stature.

It is late in coming into leaf, and unless the advent of summer is somewhat warm, it wears a bare and exceptional appearance by the side of other trees, arrayed in their bright suits of green. As its shoots continue to grow to a late period in the year, they require a more protracted summer to ripen them than can be obtained in most situations in this country.

Seen at its best, when about ten or twelve years of age, it has a delightful appearance, producing racemes of white and yellowish hue, which are very beautiful and fragrant. It seldom, however, blooms abundantly for many years in succession, being very precarious in this respect, and much influenced by the weather and seasons.

The earliest and best sheltered situations must therefore be chosen in which to plant it, where it will put on its most ornamental and attractive guise. Although it grows very rapidly during the first five years of its existence, yet from its inability to mature its shoots in this climate, they are unable to resist the frost when it comes, so that from a third to half of the extremities of the young ones are cut off, which reduces its otherwise luxuriant growth to a merely average one. The case is, however, somewhat different in specially warm positions. In the rich, dry, and well sheltered soils of North America it grows rapidly and reaches a considerable height; and even in this country, when its shoots are cut off very much during its infancy, which causes it to be branchy, it has a natural tendency to grow erect.

The locust tree is mostly raised from seeds, which generally ripen by the end of October, but the best are imported from America. It can also be raised by cuttings of the roots.

The seed-beds should be composed of light friable soil, which has been thoroughly well drained, but not made rich, unless in a southern county, where the climate is peculiarly well suited for its growth. The seeds, after being first soaked in water, should be sown in early spring, about two inches apart, covered with half an inch depth of soil, and the beds should be formed where they will get the largest amount of sunshine. The plants will make their appearance early in summer, and grow from one-and-a-half to two feet in height during the first season, seldom ripening their tops sufficiently when of a larger size, which is the chief reason why their early growth should not be too much stimulated by richly-manured land.

At one year old the plants should be removed from the seed-bed and transplanted into nursery lines two feet apart, the plants themselves standing about a foot, or a little less, asunder. Remaining in nursery lines for one or two years, they will commonly range from five to six feet high. They are then fit for being permanently placed out, which, as before said, should be in the warmest and most sheltered situations.

The timber is remarkable for strength and durability even when young, and for this purpose is esteemed for posts and for similar uses, but it seldom attains a large size, the trees rarely exceeding a foot in diameter when grown under the most favourable conditions.

As coppice it becomes feeble after being lopped pretty often, and does not answer as underwood. In situations of exposure the wood becomes brittle and is easily broken by the wind. In very exceptional situations, favourable to its growth, the tree has been known to attain a height of seventy feet, with a trunk whose diameter has been four feet; but such examples are extremely rare.

20. **THE PLANE TREE** (*Platanus*).—This tree is very often confounded with the great maple, or sycamore (*Acer pseudo-platanus*), popularly called the plane tree in Scotland, but it is entirely different, the genus comprehending only two species, the Eastern and Western plane, which are chiefly cultivated in this country as ornamental

trees, the foliage being more beautiful, perhaps, than any other both species attaining a very large size in their native *habitat*, the East of Europe and the West of Asia and of North America respectively.

The round balls in which the seeds are contained, and which hang from the tree suspended by long slender thread-like stalks, give it a very unique appearance, forming a striking feature at all seasons of the year; and in situations favourable to their growth no timber tree exceeds them in magnitude or beauty.

There is one drawback, however, to their cultivation, in their leaves being liable to be cut off by the late frosts, immediately after the expansion of the buds; and the same difficulty is experienced in this climate in the ripening of the young wood as in the case of the locust tree, our summers not being long enough to perfect it sufficiently to endure the frosts of winter.

The *P. orientalis*, or Eastern plane, is said to have been introduced into Britain about the middle of the sixteenth century, being most commonly met with in the East of Europe and West of Asia. Its wide-spreading branches present an imposing appearance, the leaves being five-lobed, palmate, with the divisions lanceolate. On young, vigorous shoots they are frequently met with a foot broad and ten inches long, but in old trees they seldom attain more than half these dimensions.

It blossoms in May, and ripens its seeds in October in favourable seasons. When the seeds are taken from the round balls which contain them, which are broken up for the purpose, they should be sifted, in order to separate them from the cottony substance with which they are blended, and put aside till the following March, when they should be sown in beds prepared after the manner previously described.

The seeds require but little covering, but they should be pressed well into the surface of the ground to keep them in position, and be kept moist, by covering the beds over with branches of trees, leaves, or some light litter which is not of too close a nature. The best method of propagation is, however, to raise trees from layers, by topping a plant over at the surface of the ground, so that a stool is readily formed which will throw out young shoots. These are bent down into the earth to the depth of three or four inches, with their extremities pointed upwards in the same manner as that described with the elm. This task should be performed in winter, or early spring, when they will take root and be ready for removal in the

November following, when the young shoots, the produce of the preceding summer, should take the place of those removed.

The plants are often four or five feet high when only one year old, transplanted from layers, when they can either be planted out, or kept another year in the nursery.

The plane likes a deep, rich, soft soil; and it is found, in all those instances where the tree has attained an unusual size, that its roots have had access to water, and, without being confined, to do well it needs shelter. It will not flourish at a great elevation, but in valleys near the banks of rivers the tree may often be seen at its best.

WESTERN PLANE.

In a suitable climate it forms a very handsome and appropriate tree for shading public walks and promenades; and in squares and streets its horizontal branches and large foliage, while excluding sunshine and rain, are yet favourable to the admission of gentle breezes, which put into motion its large leaves and produce the most agreeable effect.

The Greeks and Romans were most enthusiastic in the cultivation of the plane tree. The groves of Epicurus and around the schools of Athens were planted with the plane; as were also the groves of Academus, in which Plato delivered his celebrated discourses; and travellers in the East are all unanimous in their praises of its beauty. On the banks of the Bosphorus may be seen at the present time many trees of enormous size, some of them of a very great age.

21. **THE WESTERN PLANE** (*P. occidentalis*).—This tree was introduced into Britain from North America about two hundred and fifty years ago. It abounds in the fertile valleys along the course of the great rivers of Virginia and Pennsylvania, and on the banks of the Ohio, and neighbouring districts. Its appearance very much resembles that of the Eastern plane, its leaves being large and lobed and somewhat downy underneath, but its seed balls are smoother than the Oriental species.

It is a more rapidly growing tree than the *P. orientalis*, but is not so hardy, and, as in the case of several other kinds of trees which have been introduced into this country from others where the summers are of longer duration than English ones, its shoots seldom become matured at their extremities, and in consequence die back from the effects of frost.

It may be raised from cuttings, or propagated by layers; the method followed being the same pursued as in the case of the Oriental species; and notwithstanding the effects produced upon it by the frost, the finest specimens of the plane to be met with in this country are of this species; trees having attained the height of eighty feet in twenty years, in favourable situations, when growing near a pond, to which the roots have had access.

Its habit of growth is, for its young shoots to proceed in a zigzag direction. In a cold spring it assumes a scorched appearance, which it throws off as soon as summer weather definitely sets in, and clothes itself in the most beautiful verdure, which affords an abundant, embowering shade.

22. **THE SPANISH CHESTNUT TREE** (*Castanea vesca*) is also often called the "sweet" chestnut, to distinguish it from the horse-chestnut. It is supposed to have been introduced into Britain by the Romans, but it only ripens its fruit in the southern portions of the kingdom.

It is a handsome tree, forming an effective ornament for the lawn or park; but is more tender than the oak, and seldom equals its height or diameter under mutually favourable conditions.

It grows best in a deep sandy loam, or a rich gravelly soil, where the sub-soil is open and dry, its leaves being broad and long, dark green and glossy, strongly veined and serrated. In favourable situations its usual growth, (after having taken good root and fairly started), is at the rate of three feet yearly for the first eight or ten years, and in a close plantation in a favourable climate it rises with a clear trunk from fifty to sixty feet.

In exposed situations, or upon wet retentive soils, it spreads near the surface of the ground, and seldom ripens the extremities of its young shoots sufficiently to resist the inevitable frost.

The wood of the Spanish chestnut possesses the unusual property of being more valuable when young than when it is ripened by age, the timber deteriorating in quality after the tree has reached fifty or sixty years. In the young tree the sap, or outer wood, soon changes into heartwood, which causes it to be valuable for posts and fences, and other applications where it comes into contact with the ground, or is likely to be exposed to an alternate wet and dry condition.

Full-grown chestnut timber is often loose and deficient in compactness, the annual layers of the wood inclining to separate from one another into flakes, but when sound is useful for special purposes.

Although not very highly esteemed in this country as a timber tree, it is appreciated as coppice, for which it is often used, making capital underwood, and springing freely when lopped over. Its rapid growth and dense foliage also cause it to be very appropriate as a screen fence, where one may be needed. The bark of the chestnut is only worth half that of the oak.

There are several varieties, which are cultivated either as fruit-bearing trees, or for ornamental purposes, besides the *Castanea vesca*, as *C. americana*, which has broader leaves than the common tree; *C. variegata*, which is marked with yellow and white streaks; *C. asplenifolia*, *C. glauca*, *C. glabra*, &c.

Some writers are of opinion that the chestnut s ndigenous to this country, but the probabilities are very much against this supposition. Although not very subject to disease, it not only fails to ripen its fruit in situations which are not highly favourable for its development, but it is very much affected by unfavourable seasons, which would not be the case were it a native of Britain.

The kinds cultivated in France for the sake of their fruit, which is large and farinaceous, are termed *les marrons*, which emit an aromatic perfume when roasted in the ordinary manner. These are generally propagated by grafting, as the seeds cannot be depended upon for reproducing the original variety.

The Spanish chestnut is usually raised from seed which has been grown in this country, as many of the imported nuts are kiln-dried for the sake of keeping. They are sometimes sown in October and November, when the young trees will make their appearance in April, but they will require protection from the frost. In districts where late frosts prevail it is customary to sow them early in spring instead of late in the autumn, when the plants will come in the middle or at the end of May, when they will in all probability escape. The seeds are sometimes sown in drills about a foot and a half apart, the nuts lying in them about three inches asunder; but the usual method is in beds four feet in width, covering the seed with an inch depth of soil. One bushel of seed is sufficient for a bed thirty yards long.

Too rich a soil is not good for the young chestnut tree. It stimulates a late growth, when the young wood will not be ripened sufficiently to stand the effects of frost, and its habit will consequently become branchy, from losing its top. The plants are sometimes lifted from the seed-bed at one year, but more frequently at two years old, and planted out into nursery lines, sixteen inches asunder, the plants standing six inches from one another. If a greater space than this is allowed, they are apt to grow crooked and branchy, and not make straight trees.

After remaining two years in nursery lines the plants will commonly attain the height of from two to three feet, which is the size usually made use of for plantations. If required of a larger size, they must be transplanted every two years, increasing the space betwixt them upon each removal. Any time during October and March, in open weather, is suitable for this to be done.

MAPLE.

As a large-growing tree, the chestnut is very ornamental in appearance, its handsome green leaves changing into a mellow yellow in autumn, which gives it a very picturesque effect when grouped with others. The genus *Castanea* derives its name from Kastanea, a city in Pontus, in Asia.

23. **THE MAPLE** (*Acer*).—This genus includes about twenty hardy sorts, the largest and most common of which is the *Acer pseudo-platanus*, the mock plane tree, or sycamore. There are many interesting varieties of the maple, varying in size from large trees down to comparative shrubs, all of them being very handsome and attractive in appearance.

Some of them grow rapidly at a very early age, and in autumn furnish many diversified shades of yellow and scarlet, which has a very pleasing effect. Some, again, flower early, at the time of the expansion of their foliage.

The sycamore is a native of the hilly districts of Europe, being found in Switzerland, Austria, Germany, and Italy. In Scotland it is planted very largely upon reclaimed land, few deciduous trees being better adapted for standing in rough and exposed situations singly. Notwithstanding exposure to the wind, it will generally acquire for itself a large, well-balanced head, which is very useful for shelter, and it withstands the deteriorating effects of sea spray.

It blossoms in spring, and the seeds become ripe early in the following autumn, when they should be collected together and mixed with twice their quantity of sand, and placed in a pit, and sown in the following spring. The ground should only be moderately rich, but well pulverized. In rich, moist, stimulating soils, an excess of growth is encouraged, and the consequence is the young shoots are unable to bear the frost, which only happens, however, in the first year of their existence.

A similar result occurs when the seeds are sown in autumn, immediately upon being gathered. The plants make their appearance early in spring, and being tender, they are nearly certain to be cut off by the frosts. After sprinkling the seeds on the surface of the bed, from which the top soil has been removed, they should be covered to the depth of half an inch. One bushel of seed is sufficient for a bed four feet wide, and twenty-four yards long.

After having stood in the seed-bed for a year, the plants should be removed into nursery lines, standing six or eight inches from one another, the lines being two feet apart. Here they should remain for two years longer, when they will range from four to six feet in height, and are fit for planting-out. In a dry, deep, soft soil, which is the most favourable for its development, the sycamore will generally reach a height of twenty feet in ten years, and trees have been known to attain forty feet in twenty years. It grows well, however, in soils of very opposite qualities, coming into leaf early in the season, presenting a very attractive appearance in May, when its leaves are of a bright lively green. They, however, exude a moist glutinous substance, to which the dust of the roads and any atmospheric impurity adheres, which causes them to look dingy and takes off their beauty of appearance, and on this account it is not a good tree for planting by the road side, where it may be frequently seen. The largest and most common, the *Acer pseudo-platanus*, is not the most ornamental of the natural order *Aceraceæ*.

24. **THE SUGAR MAPLE** (*A. saccharinum*).—This tree is a native of North America, Nova Scotia, Canada, and New Brunswick. In this country it seldom grows above forty feet, but in its native districts it is found ranging from sixty feet high to seventy, though the diameter of its bulk is but small. Its leaves are white beneath, assuming in autumn a rich rosy tint, which are characteristic of many of the trees which have been imported to us from the North American continent, and which impart such variety to the effect of masses of foliage where trees of different orders are grouped together.

In its native districts it yields a copious flow of sap, which can be easily converted into sugar; hence its name. The sap is said to be richest in saccharine matter where the trees stand singly during a hot sunshine which has been preceded by a frosty night, and especially if the ground be covered with snow. Although sugar has been made from the trees in Britain, they have not been cultivated profitably for this purpose here, though numerous samples of maple sugar were shown at the Great Exhibition of 1851, and prizes awarded. It is, of course, valuable for this purpose to settlers in the districts where they are indigenous.

The sugar maple is propagated in the same way as the sycamore, the wood being esteemed for many purposes, especially cabinet-making, but is not durable if exposed to moisture. In old trees the marks and fibres often assume very eccentric forms, being spotted; they are much appreciated for veneers, taking the name of bird's-eye maple in common with the field maple, *A. campestris.*

MAPLE TREE.

25. **THE NORWAY MAPLE** (*Acer platanoides*).—This species includes several distinct varieties, amongst the most remarkable of which is the cut-leaved or eagle's-claw maple, which is usually propagated by grafts, or buds, on a common sycamore stock, which is the only safe way for insuring any special variety. It is quite a hardy tree, and grows very rapidly when young, its growth exceeding that of the sycamore during the first few years of its life, though ultimately it does attain a similar size.

It is propagated in the same way as the sycamore, and succeeds best in a deep, well-drained soil. Its leaves are of a fine form, with a glossy polish, and retain their bright green appearance throughout the summer, changing in autumn to various hues, in which yellow predominates.

26. **THE LARGE-LEAVED MAPLE** (*A. macrophyllum*).—This tree is also a native of the North American continent, but grows rapidly in England, and attains a large size. It was only introduced into this country at the commencement of the present century, being very ornamental, yielding beautifully marked timber, which is very valuable. Its method of propagation is by layers.

27. **THE STRIPED-BARKED, OR SNAKE-BARKED MAPLE** (*A. striatum*).—This tree is remarkable for its bark being marked longitudinally with black and white stripes, and is also a native of

North America, not attaining a very great height, which seldom exceeds thirty feet.

It is usually propagated by being grafted on the common sycamore, but is sometimes raised from imported seeds. The wood, which is white, is appreciated for cabinet work. The tree, at all periods of its growth, presents a highly ornamental appearance.

28. **THE RED, OR SCARLET MAPLE** (*A. rubrum*).—This tree produces red blossoms early in summer, or late in spring, and is also a native of North America. It thrives better in a moist situation than any of the others, but likes a deep, rich soil. As it is difficult to rear from seed, it is mostly propagated by layers. It is a low-growing tree, but produces very valuable timber, being marked in the most diversified manner.

There are also several other kinds which present a very ornamental appearance, as *A. circinatum*, with pendulous branches which in autumn are clothed with leaves which surpass in brilliancy those of the finest scarlet oaks. In the State of Oregon they may be seen forming impenetrable thickets, varying in height from twenty to forty feet. Another hardy maple is the *A. Villosum*, which has been brought to us from the Himalayas, and which attains a large size, something similar to, but superior to the sycamore.

There are also other species of this genus more or less ornamental, but they are mostly of smaller growth.

29. **THE WALNUT TREE** (*Juglans*).—There are several species of the walnut tree cultivated in England, the common kind being held in the greatest estimation, on account of the fruit it bears. The flowers of the genus are unisexual, being both produced on one plant.

30. **THE ROYAL, OR COMMON WALNUT** (*J. regia*).—This tree was introduced into England from Persia about the middle of the sixteenth century, and rapidly became a favourite, as it attains a large size as a timber tree, being of great duration, and, when planted in sufficient space, attaining an elegant and picturesque appearance, throwing out sturdy limbs, resembling the oak somewhat in its ramifications. Its timber is white and soft when young, but as it advances in age it becomes dark and solid, beautifully veined and shaded, of a light brown colour and black blended; when seasoned, neither being subject to crack nor to warp, being preferred for many kinds of cabinet work, for gun-stocks, &c. The roots of the trees when boiled yield a brown dye, which becomes fixed in fibrous substances, such as hair and wool, as well as wood. It blossoms in May, and its fruit ripens in the following autumn.

It is propagated from the nuts, or seed, which fall to the ground on becoming ripe, and part from their outer husks. They may be sown in winter or early spring, in drills a few inches from one another, and covered with two inches depth of soil, which should be a dry and early one, otherwise the shoots will not get sufficiently matured to stand the frost. A dry sandy soil, somewhat poor in quality, is better to raise young plants in than a rich one; for, although they are smaller in size than those which are reared in a rich soil, the latter in most instances will lose their tops, unless standing in a very warm situation.

The nuts vegetate during the first season, and the young plant forms a strong tap-root. They should therefore be raised from the seed-bed at one year old (or at most two years) and the extremities of their tap-roots be cut off, so as to produce that bushiness of fibre which is so essential for the growth of all young trees. As the plants are apt to suffer from frost soon after making their first appearance above ground, the drills should be protected by branches of fir, or other suitable cover. Transplantation should be continued every second or third year, allowing the plants upon their removal sufficient space to grow in, according to their size. They will grow rapidly in a deep dry soil where the climate is good, and will attain a height of twenty feet in twelve years, when they usually begin to bear fruit, and the growth of a tree becomes slower, and its habit more spreading.

Upon poor surface soils, but where there is a good sub-soil, the walnut is more likely to succeed than any other tree, throwing out a strong tap-root more vigorous even than that of the oak, and as a timber tree it maintains a good head in windy and exposed situations, where it is less likely to be overturned if raised by seed where it stands without transplantation. Cultivated, however, for the sake of its fruit, it is more prolific for being transplanted. Trees which have not been transplanted do not ripen their fruit so early as those which have been put out into nursery lines, which, it is thought, is owing to the fact that their roots range nearer to the surface of the ground, and so benefit by the influence of the sunshine. Trees also of a great age ripen their fruit better in a cold climate than the young ones in the same district.

The roots striking deeply into the ground, causes it to be well adapted for a hedge-row tree, but it is not often found occupying such a situation in this country, though commonly used for this purpose on the Continent, as it does not interfere with the cultivation of the neighbouring fields. Upon fairly good soils, incumbent upon chalk or gravel, the walnut generally succeeds remarkably well, and in such situations frequently yields large crops of fruit.

31. **THE BLACK WALNUT OF AMERICA** (*J. nigra*).—The leaves of this species are about twice as long as those of the common walnut, being composed of six or eight pairs of opposite leaflets, with a single terminal leaflet, which emit a strong but agreeable

aromatic odour, the same as the common description. It is readily raised from seed, which is imported from America, the method of cultivation being the same as that adopted with the common species, which it exceeds in robustness of growth, and flourishes in England with the same vigour which marks its progress in its native country.

As a fruit tree, however, it is inferior to the common kind, and being later in ripening, it is only resorted to as a timber tree, or for standing in isolated positions, as for the adornment of a lawn, where it will assume a beautiful spreading habit, provided the soil be good.

The timber is of a very dark colour, handsomely grained, and takes a high polish, being in request for many of the higher articles of cabinet work and furniture.

32. **THE GREY WALNUT TREE** (*J. cinerea*).—This species is also a native of America, being propagated in the same manner as the black walnut, to which it bears a strong resemblance, though it is less commonly met with. All the species of the American hickory, which are held in high estimation on that continent, are comprehended in the same natural order, that of *Juglandaceæ.*

33. **BROAD-LEAVED TREES FOR ELEVATED SITUATIONS.**—The broad-leaved trees we have enumerated are those which generally prefer good soils, and mostly do not thrive in elevated positions. Those adapted for great altitudes, of the broad-leaved species of the most hardy kinds, being the mountain ash, sycamore, service tree, trembling poplar, Scotch elm, goat willow, birch, ash, and alder.

34. **PRICES OF TWO-YEAR OLD PLANTS.**—We have described the various methods of rearing the young trees which have been enumerated, but two-year old transplanted plants may be purchased at a very reasonable price, where time is an object, at about the following rates:—

Spanish chestnut	40*s*.	per 1000.
Oak	25*s*.	"
Ash	25*s*.	"
Sycamore	25*s*.	"
Birch	25*s*.	"
Elm (Scotch)	25*s*.	"
Beech	20*s*.	"

Large numbers are reared by nurserymen, who make a distinct branch of business of raising these trees, birch plants of a year old, when about six inches high, selling from 4*s*. to 6*s*. per 1000.

CHAPTER II.

TREES WHICH GROW BEST IN MOIST SITUATIONS.

The Goat Willow—The White or Huntingdon Willow—The Bedford Willow—Willow Embankments—Ornamental Willows—The Alder—The Poplar Tree—Grey Poplar—The Aspen—White Poplar—The Lombardy Poplar—The Balsam Poplar—Black Italian Poplar—The Ontario Poplar—The Lime Tree—The American Lime Tree—The Horse-chestnut—The Scarlet-flowering Horse-chestnut, &c.

The trees which succeed best in moist situations, or near to water more or less, are the willow, alder, poplar, lime, and horse-chestnut. Fast-growing, or soft-wooded trees, if the land is well trenched in the first place, will grow on dry soils, and even appear to flourish for a time, but they do not attain their full vigour on sandy uplands, and some show signs of not being at home, not attaining the full luxuriance and beauty of which they are capable.

At the highest altitudes, and in the driest exposures, the willow is occasionally found among the few plants of ligneous form, being extremely hardy and tenacious of life when young. In some places, when a close plantation of fir, larch, or other timber has been felled, which does not spring again from the root, as oak or Spanish chestnut, it is sometimes found difficult to form a cover of any kind or vegetation, and for this purpose willows are useful, especially in the form of nurses for establishing more valuable trees. In this capacity, however, they require the attention of a forester or experienced person, being apt to confine and smother the other trees with which they are associated.

35. **THE WILLOW** (natural order, *Salicaceæ*).—The genus *Salix*

comprehends many diversified species, natives of various parts of the world, ranging from low-growing osiers to large trees, which are sometimes eighty feet in height. From twenty to thirty distinct species are natives of Britain, but these, again, have been divided into a great number of varieties, the more prominent kinds having become hybridized, producing intermediate varieties without number.

It is also very apt to change its appearance according to soil and situation, and at certain seasons of the year; and a good deal of confusion exists as to sub-varieties, though the prominent species are readily enough recognised. As timber trees, there are three important varieties indigenous in this country, which are very hardy, and attain a certain size in almost any soil or situation, preferring, as we have before stated, a moist one.

36. **THE GOAT WILLOW, OR SALLOW** (*S. caprea*).—This tree and its varieties are among the broadest-leaved of the willow family, being often found growing naturally in waste ground, especially in cold and marshy situations. In rich, moist ground, a two-year-old seedling plant will throw out shoots three or four feet long, and invariably ripens the wood it has made, even in the most unfavourable seasons, to their extremities.

The goat-willow will often attain a height of forty or fifty feet, with a trunk from four-and-a-half feet to six feet in circumference. Near the sea it affords valuable shelter, and will stand the exposure of maritime situations, the timber being considered the best of any of the willows. It is a valuable tree for coppice, and may be cut down every three or four years, during which period no other tree will produce so large a quantity of wood.

It is also a handsome tree as well, the dark brown glossy bark of its vigorous young shoots in spring-time contrasting with its prominent white buds, while the male plant produces a profusion of handsome catkins, which, in the early part of the opening season, give to it a very gay appearance, and cause it to be extremely ornamental, well worthy of being cultivated as a decorative tree, in shape of a standard in a shrubbery, where its beautiful yellow catkins will show to great advantage.

It is propagated by cuttings; strong one-year shoots are selected, and formed into sets of fourteen or sixteen inches long, and inserted ten or twelve inches into the ground. They generally strike readily enough, but where the ground is not of a good quality, or has not been properly prepared, it is the best plan to use rooted plants.

37. **THE WHITE, OR HUNTINGDON WILLOW** (*S. alba*).—There is no tree, if we except the grey poplar, which attains so

great a size during the first twenty or thirty years of its existence as the Huntingdon willow, in this country. In the soils and situations most favourable to its growth it is often found sixty and seventy feet high at that age, being more frequently planted as a timber tree than any other willow. It also makes a capital pollard, and forms good coppice. Its year-old shoots are very tough and strong, but being full of laterals, it is not adapted for the better kinds of basket-making—a use to which the twigs of the willows are often applied—being suited only for the coarser sorts.

38. **THE BEDFORD WILLOW, OR RUSSELL'S** (*S. Russelliana*), which takes its name from the Duke of Bedford, who first brought it into notice, is considered one of the best willow-trees in cultivation, attaining a very large size; trees being seen which are fifty feet high, with trunks of three feet diameter.

HUNTINGDON WILLOW.

The three species we have mentioned are all very hardy, and will attain a certain size in soil of almost any description, but rich, deep earth in the vicinity of water develops them to the greatest perfection. The timber of the willow is white, soft, and light, which causes it to be well adapted for various agricultural purposes, such as sheep hurdles, the handles of rakes or scythes, &c., and for any purpose where lightness of weight is desirable. As timber, its chief advantage consists in its not being easily splintered, which renders its planks very useful as linings for carts or barrows, where it will not receive damage from the fall of hard substances, such as stones, casks of liquor, or other weighty objects, upon it.

39. **WILLOW EMBANKMENTS.**—Willows may be readily formed into embankments for resisting the encroachment of streams and rivers. Branches of the different species, when cut between October and April, are put framewise from the channel of the water to the top of the flow-bank, with a gentle slope, the larger timbers being interwoven with the smaller branches, the whole being covered over a few inches in depth with the ordinary soil of the banks, sand or gravel. The branches readily produce numerous fibres, and create a surface vegetation in a form effectual for resisting the encroachment of the water. By being lopped

every year, the willows form a permanent embankment, and the loose materials, as it were, become consolidated.

40. **ORNAMENTAL WEEPING WILLOWS.**—There are a great number of ornamental weeping willows, one of the handsomest being *S. Babylonica.* Being a native of Asia and the north of Africa, it is somewhat tender, and it is only in the most genial situations that it ripens its young twigs to their extremities. Unlike most of the willow varieties, it does not grow freely from cuttings, and should therefore be propagated by layers. The American weeping willow is a graceful and highly ornamental tree, but being a plant of somewhat feeble growth, for the purpose of exhibiting it in its most attractive form, it is usual to graft it upon the top of a stout stem of a free-growing kind, such as the goat willow. Its long slender stems droop gracefully downwards, and are agitated by the softest breeze.

A drooping variety of the *S. caprea* has also been a good deal cultivated of late years. The male plants of the purple, black, and yellow osiers form very ornamental trees of low stature—especially when displaying their catkins in profusion—the gaiety and richness of their early blossoms indicating the advent of approaching summer.

Of the dwarf willows, or osiers, however, we shall speak again, the most approved kinds of which are the *S. viminalis*, *S. rubra*, *S. forbyana*, &c., which we shall treat upon under the heading of "Osier beds."

WHITE WILLOW.

41. **THE ALDER** (*Alnus glutinosa*).—The alder may be considered as a most useful adjunct in reclaiming meadow lands that are partially flooded, or even continuously so, in low-lying situations. This is effected by ridging that portion of the soil over which the water flows in summer-time, and planting young alder trees on the ridge. In the course of a few years the roots will get firmly established in the ground, and, by the fall of the leaves, the soil will gradually get firm and dry. It is the most aquatic tree growing in this country, and in damp situations, near the edges of rivers, it frequently attains a height of sixty feet. It reaches maturity when at fifty or sixty years of age, when it should be cut down, if timber is the object in view; but while growing it supplies a large quantity of faggot-wood for hurdles and other useful appliances.

The alder, being seen frequently growing on the banks of streams and in moist situations, used in old times to bear the character of a tree which *created* dampness; but the reverse is the case, it having a tendency to dry up moisture, which it absorbs into its own constitution. It will frequently succeed well in situations where other kinds of trees refuse to grow, and is thus often made useful as a hedge plant in the fen districts, and being quick-growing, it is sometimes resorted to near newly-built residences destitute of trees, where it will readily make a show, while other trees, of a more valuable description, are growing.

It is not, however, a good-looking tree, though, being mostly found in the neighbourhood of streams and rivulets, it is often credited with a portion of that beauty which, on the whole, belongs to certain situations and is the effect of natural scenery, of which the alder is only an accompaniment, its aspect being plain and even somewhat gloomy.

ALDER.

Its propagation used to be by layers and suckers, but this practice has given way to the plan of sowing the seeds, which are contained in small cones, which become ripe about the middle or end of October. As these cones are apt to get mouldy, they should be spread over the floor of a room in which a fire is frequently kept up, to the depth of six inches or so, where they should remain till the beginning of April, being well stirred over in the meantime. They should then be threshed, sifted, and cleaned, and slightly moistened for twenty-four hours with milk and warm water, which is best done on the floor of a barn or outhouse.

The seeds should be planted in moist meadow land that has been dug over evenly and finely (but not raked), in beds of the usual width, *i.e.*, four feet, with alleys of twelve inches wide, for the convenience of walking between the beds. The seeds should be sown on the surface, as thickly as they can lie without touching one another, and then trod in carefully with the feet, so as to make the surface of the bed flat and even. By this method the seeds will become thoroughly incorporated with the land, and will not become so dry in the summer-time as if the top of the beds had been smoothly raked, the seeds not requiring an even cover, but merely to be blinded, as it were.

In good moist land, the plants by the ensuing November will be nine inches high, or probably even more, sometimes reaching a foot, when they should be lifted from the seed-bed and planted in nursery lines, a foot and a half apart, the plants standing six inches from each other in the rows. After remaining two years in this position they will be fit for planting out permanently.

The alder thrives best when planted separately by the margins of streams or rivers, in the soil of which it delights, and the land only requires digging to be ready for the reception of trees. Holes should be dug with a common garden spade, nine inches in depth, between November and March, at four feet distance between each, and as they increase in size the intermediate ones should be cut out, the wood thus obtained being of considerable value, first as faggot-wood, and afterwards as poles, according to the growth and age of the trees, and the object and intent of the plantation.

Thinning and pruning should also be performed, keeping in mind that the leaves exercise the most important functions of the growing tree, and too many branches must not be removed. Woodmen who ought to know their business better, and who aim at producing a large trunk, often strip off the side branches, with the idea that they are developing the bole, and so the more quickly growing timber, forgetting, or not knowing, that a large trunk cannot be grown without branches. At the same time, a side-shoot which is likely to interfere with the supremacy of the leading branches should be removed while young.

This principle of course applies to every description of tree, and a skilful man will carefully scrutinise and weigh in his mind the most judicious treatment to be resorted to in the case of each individual tree, so as to lop off those branches which will be best taken away, and yet leave sufficient to be the means of developing and maturing the sap of the tree, so as to build up its entire fabric.

The alder is a good tree to act as a nurse for more valuable ones planted by the sea-side, which, without some such protection as they will afford, would not otherwise be able to be reared during the tender stages of their early youth. Its timber is useful to cabinet-makers, last-makers, &c., and is used for purposes where white and soft wood is required, along with the willow, generally fetching from sixteen to eighteen pence per cubic foot; but as the root end of the alder is often finely veined this portion generally fetches a much higher price.

The wood is subject to the attack of insects, and to remedy this, when it can be done, immediately after felling, the finer pieces are immersed in a pit of water, dug in a peat bog, for two months; the water being impregnated with a bushel or two of lime. Wood prepared in this way, when French polished, bears some resemblance to mahogany, though of a duller colour, and in its usual state it is fit for the same purpose to which willow timber is applied, in the lining of carts, &c., and the stout branches for handles of agricultural implements. For hop-poles, however, they are not suitable, being very inferior to the ash or Spanish-chestnut.

Like other young trees, alder plants can be purchased at a very cheap rate from the nurserymen, who sell them a foot high for half a dozen shillings or so per thousand. In country districts dyers use the products of the alder in their trade. If cut in the spring, the shoots dye a cinnamon colour, and the catkins produce a green.

42. **THE POPLAR** (*Populus*).—This familiar genus of deciduous trees, of the natural order *Salicaceæ*, embraces many species, comprehending different varieties of form and foliage indigenous to all parts of the globe, all of which are remarkable for the quickness of their growth, which causes the tree to be extremely valuable for bare situations, where trees are wanted; and although many of them are short-lived, they can be made extremely useful for shelter or embellishment while slower-growing trees are approaching maturity, when their services may ultimately be dispensed with. It produces unisexual flowers on separate plants, and although destitute of the beauty of form which distinguishes many other trees, yet may often be used to advantage when interspersed with different kinds.

43. **THE GRAY POPLAR** (*P. canescens*).—This variety thrives best in moist soils, and is remarkable for producing lateral shoots nearly equal in strength to the top one, at a very early age, and on this account is often resorted to to stand with other trees, with a view to their removal when the more valuable kinds have become established. When cut down at an early period of its growth it shoots freely, but at an advanced age it springs vigorously from the roots, and produces a great number of suckers, which causes it to be unfit for some situations.

It is a native of Britain, growing freely, and forming a large spreading tree. It flowers in April, and makes itself conspicuous by its profusion of catkins two or three inches in length. The seeds generally ripen in June, from which it is occasionally raised, but the tree is best propagated by layers, which is done by lopping a plant over at the surface of the ground, which produces a number of young shoots, which are readily formed into a stool. The young plants are bent down into the earth during winter or early spring, with their extremities in an upright position (in the same way as before described), which will become rooted by the end of the following autumn, when they should be planted out into nursery lines.

After being one year transplanted, the young trees will be often five or six feet high, and be ready for planting out. Its timber is soft and white, being much of the same character as that of the willow, but cannot be grown longer than forty or fifty years, as the trunk is apt to decay in the middle. Its wood is chiefly used for packing-cases, and takes the place of inferior deal for common purposes. The large packing-cases which come from abroad, in which dry goods are sent to us from France, Germany, and other European countries, are mostly made of poplar, its timber being soft and light. Being less likely to catch fire than deal, it is also frequently used as flooring near fire-places, by builders who study such matters; while, as it does not warp, it is also well adapted for the doors of barns, &c., and is appropriate for the work of the carver.

Planted by itself in a rich, moist soil, it will rise from thirty to forty feet in ten years; ultimately making a clean trunk, producing a great bulk of timber in a short space of time.

44. **THE TREMBLING-LEAVED POPLAR, OR ASPEN** (*P. tremula*).—This is a beautiful, round-headed tree, of elegant appearance, tall in proportion to its size, which grows very rapidly, and is also extremely hardy. It will grow luxuriantly in almost any kind of soil when young, even if dry and sandy, as well as in stiff, wet clay.

It is indigenous to Britain, and is common in most elevated districts throughout Europe and Asia, being often found associated in Scotland with the natural birch, where its young shoots are eaten greedily by cattle and sheep. The roots of the tree spread very much over the surface of the ground, and it is, on this account, somewhat objectionable in certain situations; as they are apt to form a jungle, from its propensity to spring from its roots. In Sweden and Germany these are regularly used for cattle in both a green and a dried state.

In ordinary soils the growth of the aspen, during the first ten years of its life, is at the rate of three feet annually. Being of a vivid bright green, its foliage forms an agreeable contrast to that of most trees during the summer; and few trees present a more engaging appearance in the landscape. Standing alone as a lawn tree, it assumes a very interesting character, being often of a pendulous form. After the first frosts of autumn its leaves change to a mellow ripened hue, which ultimately merge into a bright yellow. When it has attained a certain age the trunk becomes of an ash colour, and, with tasteful arrangement, can be made to produce an excellent arboretical effect on the borders of plantations and other situations, as on the sloping sides of a forest.

Upon the sides of slopes, when the altitude is not too great for varied arborescent vegetation, the trembling of its leaves is very conspicuous, from the construction of the leaf and leaf-stalk, its leaves being round and smooth, standing on long slender foot-stalks, which are agitated by the most gentle airs, so that their quivering is distinctly heard even in the calmest weather, the murmuring notes being very delightful to lovers of nature's music.

The seeds of *P. tremula* ripen in summer, and may be immediately sown; but propagation by suckers or layers is the quickest plan of raising trees. Cuttings from the roots grow quickly, but not cuttings from the branches, like most of the other poplars, and the timber is similar in its nature to that of most others of the species.

45. **THE WHITE POPLAR** (*P. alba*).—This variety bears a strong resemblance to the gray poplar, but its leaves are of darker green above and more white beneath, which is plainly seen when they are agitated by the wind. It is supposed to have been brought over here from Flanders at an early period, and is not a native of Britain.

The handsomest known variety of this tree is that distinguished as the Egyptian poplar, the leaves of which are yet more dark green above, and the whitest beneath, of any of the species; its growth, however, being far less vigorous than that of the common variety.

The *P. alba* is sometimes subject to an atmospheric disease somewhat resembling the potato blight, from which the gray poplar (*P. canescens*) is much more exempt. In instances where both kinds of trees have stood closely together, the latter has been quite free from it, while the former has been very much affected.

46. **THE FASTIGIATE, OR LOMBARDY POPLAR** (*P. fastigiata*).—The Lombardy poplar is a native of Italy, abounding on the banks of the Po, and was imported into England about the middle of the eighteenth century, and soon became popular throughout Britain, from the facility with which it could be raised.

Throughout a great part of the Continent the tree is almost universal, and long tracts of monotonous flat country are only broken in uniformity by the continuous rows of poplars, which make another species of uniformity of their own. It is the universal divider of fields there, and is frequently made use of for fences, which are formed by planting two-year-old plants, which at that age stand six or seven feet high, in straight lines about six inches apart. These are connected by a horizontal rod placed at a height of three feet from the ground, and thus a good fence is produced in one season.

The example thus furnished to us by our continental neighbours is one well worthy of being imitated by those who want a good hedge in an incredibly short space of time, but it is one that is rarely resorted to by agriculturists in this country.

The Lombardy poplar is a capital tree for town situations, as it endures the effects of smoke almost better than any other tree, and stands in a very narrow space, springing rapidly, and assuming its natural form from a very early period, wearing its characteristic appearance from its youth upwards.

It is distinguished from every other species by its upright growth, with its branches gathered closely around its trunk, assuming a taper shape, being the most upright of all the deciduous trees. Trees of this species are not uncommonly met with on the Continent ranging 150 feet in height, and they have been known to grow to 125 feet in fifty years. Planted in agricultural districts its shade is but little injurious to the neighbouring crops, its entire top bending to the breeze.

It grows vigorously in any kind of soil during its infancy, but to attain the large size we have mentioned it must stand in a rich soil, and its roots have access to water. As it advances in years the trunk becomes deeply furrowed and it is not apt to produce undergrowths, which is an objectionable feature in some kinds of poplars.

It can be propagated very easily by cuttings, which will grow as speedily as any description of willows, and as they soon rise to a great height, a handsome screen may be established in a very short time, forming a wall of living verdure.

Forming a striking contrast in shape to the round-headed trees, this variety may often be advantageously introduced in landscape decoration, with the result of changing and improving the features of any scene which is without them. A tree or two judiciously placed near the end of a barn, or outbuilding, will hide an objectionable object which may be too near to be pleasant to the eye, and which thus may be advantageously screened. Clumps skilfully planted in the proximity of other trees, especially when the vision rests upon them at a considerable distance, relieve the monotony of the aspect, and break the continuity of the sky line in an agreeable manner.

Its wood is soft and light, and not of much value beyond its adaptability for packing-cases and for those uses where lightness is an advantage.

47. **THE BALSAM POPLAR** (*P. balsamifera*).—This is a very ornamental species, which in early spring bursts out into leaves of a pale yellow colour, emitting a rich balsamic fragrance, which diffuses its odours around. The young wood it makes is of a rich chestnut colour, and the large buds produced upon it are encased in a glutinous balsam.

In America, from whence it has been imported into England, it attains a height of eighty feet, but in this country it is not remarkable for its altitude, growing vigorously for a few years only during its youth. Its leaves mostly become dark green as the season advances, there being several varieties, which differ from each other in the size and shape of their leaves, in their manner of growth, and the time at which they expand their foliage.

The trunk has an ash-coloured bark, and the tree will grow in any description of soil, preferring that which is soft, rich, moist, and moderately sheltered. The different varieties may be easily propagated either by cuttings or suckers, its habit being to produce the latter.

48. **BLACK ITALIAN OR NECKLACE-BEARING POPLAR** (*P. monilifera*).—This is a rapidly-growing tree of a similar nature to the gray poplar, with which it should be associated, unless planted by itself, when it generally succeeds the best. Abounding in wild

BLACK POPLAR.

rocky ground, and on the margins of lakes in Canada, it is sometimes called the Canadian poplar, its usual height there being seventy or eighty feet. Single specimens in good land in this country reach a still greater height, and on rich moist soil it becomes a timber tree of considerable size in comparatively a very few years. It also grows freely on very poor soil, provided its roots have access to water.

Its growth is more vigorous than that of the Lombardy poplar, from which it is easily distinguished, when a plant, by its leaves being broader and its young shoots ribbed, particularly towards the extremities, and of a much darker colour. Its side shoots take a wider range, and do not grow so closely to the trunk. It has been known to attain the height of sixty feet at twenty-five years of age.

The poplars do not like pruning, the knife being very apt to introduce decay into their trunks, so that, in order to induce a close habit of growth in a plantation, the trees should stand a little thickly, when the confinement will induce a curtailment of the somewhat spreading habit in which the tree naturally delights to shape itself.

It can be propagated very easily by cuttings. Its timber is white and durable, if kept dry; and on that account is considered useful for flooring and other purposes, though, like that of all the other varieties, it is reckoned to be of far inferior value to deal.

49. **THE ONTARIO POPLAR** (*P. candicans*).—This tree is very similar to the balsam poplar, but grows much more vigorously, producing large heart-shaped leaves. It does not answer to grow as timber, and unless raised upon a soil which stimulates its growth and insures a healthy development of its quick-growing qualities, the branches become very brittle.

There are also many other varieties of poplars, but we have named the principal ones best worth cultivating, a number of new sorts having been lately introduced from America.

50. **THE LIME TREE, OR LINDEN.**—The *Teil tree* belongs to *Polyandria monogynia* of the Linnæan system, and of the type of the natural order *Tiliaceæ*, embracing a great number of varieties possessed of different characteristics, the principal tree of the genus being the *Tilia europæa*, or common lime. It is found growing wild in the mountainous districts of Europe, as the Alps of Switzerland, and is also a native of the north of Germany, Russia, and Sweden, as well as being found in Spain and Italy.

Found growing wild in some parts of Essex and Kent, it is said by some to be indigenous to England, but doubts are cast upon this supposition from the fact that the tree does not shed its seeds and spring up in uncultivated soil, as indigenous plants are usually in the habit of doing.

In England the seeds of the lime tree only ripen in the warmest and longest summers, and in the most favourable position for its growth and development; it being unsuitable for bleak situations or dry poor soils. The tree is, indeed, often found in the north of England, in somewhat cold districts, but although it grows, it cannot be said to flourish there, as it likes a good climate and a rich alluvial soil, or one that is deep and loamy.

Its blossoms expand in July, and are the most fragrant in hot weather, and being planted in lines along the promenades in some of the chief continental cities, the heat reflected by the pavement and surrounding buildings brings out this quality in a very marked degree.

It grows rapidly, and in appropriate situations soon assumes the

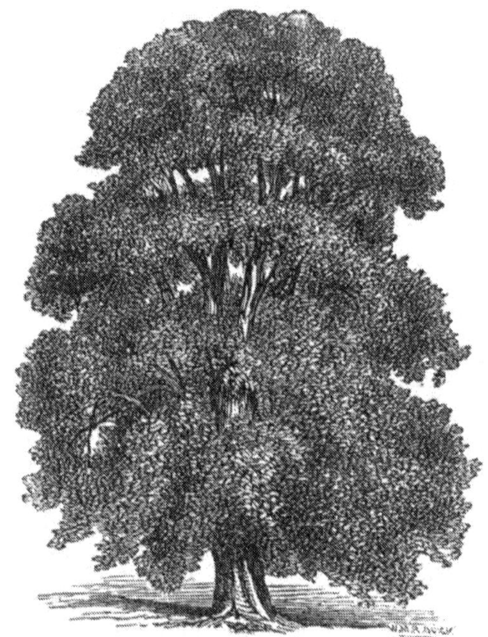

LIME.

form of a pliant, well-balanced tree, very suited for the formation of avenues, and harmonising well with cultivated grounds, to mark their boundaries or shade approaches to them. The wood is soft, of a pale yellow or white colour, and is held in estimation for such purposes as carving, to make blocks to cut leather upon and other substances, in foundries for forming moulds, and for any purpose requiring a fine surface, or where it is necessary that the wood employed does not warp. Architects find it useful for forming the models of buildings, and the inner bark furnishes materials for the manufacture of mats and the covering of packages.

In those favourable situations for the best development of its health and growth, the seeds get ripe in autumn, and may be sown in winter or spring. The method of raising plants from seeds is, however, seldom followed, as they can be obtained so much more quickly from layers, by lopping over a plant at the surface of the ground in the way which has been previously described. The shoots should be manured occasionally, and in soils that are destitute of silex it will be found of advantage to apply a few spadefuls of good sharp sand.

The shoots should be laid down in winter or early spring, and they will become well rooted and fit for removal in the November following. After three years, a stool which stands in a rich depth of compost, or vegetable mould, of the nature we have described, will produce from sixty to seventy plants a year, so that a great number may be raised by multiplying the number of stools, where a considerable quantity of plants is wanted.

The plants, when separated for removal, are generally about a couple of feet high, and they should then be planted out into nursery lines, two and a half feet apart, the plants standing fifteen or sixteen inches from one another. After standing thus for a couple of years, they will mostly attain a height of six feet, and then be fit for finally planting out.

It may, however, be successfully grown to a much larger size, and stand removal well, if it is transplanted every second year, allowing an increased space for its growth upon each removal, which has the effect of forming its roots into a fibrous condition—a point which is of the utmost consequence to bear in mind always.

It stands pruning well, and can be cut to any shape that may be required, and is therefore very serviceable as a screen fence, where such a protection may be needed, for although destitute of foliage in winter, it grows close and twiggy. It will attain a height of eighty feet in open situations, the average progress of the tree, in a rich soil in a sheltered situation, being at the rate of a couple of feet annually, for the first fifteen or twenty years of its life, under favourable circumstances, the spread of its branches equalling in diameter the number of feet contained in its height.

There are some very large lime trees to be found in various parts of the country, some ranging nearly a hundred feet in height, which are interspersed throughout some of the English parks, becoming a lofty tree, when seen at its best; its branches drooping down, and occasionally taking root in the ground; displaying, as it were, a mountain of beautiful foliage of the finest texture.

The honey produced by bees from the blossoms of the lime tree, is said to excel all other kinds in delicacy, selling for three or four times the price realized for common honey, being exclusively used for medicine, and the manufacture of liqueurs. The little town of Kowna on the river Niemans in Lithuania, which is surrounded by extensive forests of this tree, according to Loudon, furnishes this honey in considerable quantities.

51. **THE AMERICAN LIMETREE** (*Tilia Americana*).—This variety is a month later than the European variety in expanding its blossoms, and is of more robust habit, its leaves being larger, corded, acutely pointed, generally smooth and shining, and of a dark green colour. The young trees generally assume a spreading form, in the direction of their branches, the twigs being of a dark brown colour.

In America it attains a height of eighty feet, but is not very commonly met with in this country, liking a rich deep soil, the same as is found on the margins of the Canadian lakes, where the tree abounds. Its mode of propagation and treatment is the same as that followed with the common tree, the timber of both kinds resembling each other very closely. There are several varieties of this species.

The other leading sorts of the common lime tree are *alba*, the white-leaved; *microphylla*, or small-leaved; *platyphilla*, the broad-leaved; *rubra*, the red-twigged; *aurea*, the yellow-twigged; and *laciniata*, the cut-leaved; which are all European varieties.

52. **THE HORSE-CHESTNUT** (*Æsculus hippocastanum*).—The horse-chestnut attains the largest dimensions of all our flowering ornamental trees, displaying a mass of handsome blossoms which present a most beautiful appearance when in full bloom. The chestnut-trees in Bushey Park are one of the sights near London when out in blossom, and numbers of persons make a practice of going to see them every year.

HORSE CHESTNUT.

The tree rises with a straight trunk in a pyramidal form, with a large umbrageous head, clothed with fine leaves of a deep green colour, and is a beautiful object upon a lawn, in hedgerows, or for the formation of an avenue. It is thought to have been introduced into this country from the Levant about the middle of the sixteenth century, and there is no tree more useful for decorative purposes, though its timber is very inferior and possesses but little value.

The growth of the tree is somewhat remarkable, for soon after the foliage begins to expand, it makes its entire season's growth in three or four weeks at the outside. The young wood, being thus matured so early, is enabled to stand the frosts of winter, and in consequence causes the tree to be admirably well adapted for standing in unfavourable situations, where prevailing cold and wet would be likely to injure other trees.

It is, however, only in warm and sheltered situations that the tree blossoms abundantly and bears a large quantity of nuts. These become ripe about the end of October, and can be planted any time during the winter. In somewhat moist situations, where the soil is deep and rich, the nuts, as they fall from the tree, will often take root where they have dropped, in undisturbed situations.

The seed will strike in almost any kind of soil, but beds should be prepared four feet in width as usual; a deep free loam being preferable, to cause them to grow with vigour. The size of the seedlings depends a good deal upon the size and soundness of the nuts selected for use. Good large seed should therefore be carefully chosen, and placed in position upon the beds, and either rolled or beaten down with the back of a spade, to keep them in their proper position, and then covered with about an inch and a half depth of soil. A bushel of nuts will plant a bed four feet in width and twenty yards long.

After the plants have stood in the seed-bed for a year, or two years at discretion, they should be planted into nursery lines, two feet asunder, the plants standing in the rows from eight inches to a foot from one another. These should be transplanted every three years, allowing extra space for them to grow in; and, owing to the fibrous nature of the roots of the horse-chestnut, this tree will bear removal at a larger size than most species will permit.

The nuts are only used in this country for feeding deer, which pick up the fallen ones in the various parks where they abound. Containing a bitter taste, they are rejected by pigs even: but this is said to be extracted on the Continent by the use of a weak alkaline ley and they are used for feeding cattle. They are also brought into requisition there for making starch, of the component parts of which the nut contains a large quantity.

53. **THE SCARLET-FLOWERING HORSE-CHESTNUT**, &c.—This flowers at an earlier age than the common tree, being of more dwarf habit, as well as the yellow-flowering and smooth-fruited kinds, which are also of dwarf growth, known as the genus *Pavia*. These are best reproduced by grafting them upon a stock of the common variety, when they may be readily grown in sufficient numbers, as may be required.

CHAPTER III.

Trees Adapted for Thin and Poor Soils, and Elevated Situations.

The Pine Tree—The Scotch Pine—Prices of Scotch Pine Plants—Scotch Pine Seedlings for bare exposures—The Corsican Pine—Black Pine of Austria—The Stone Pine—The Weymouth Pine—The Cembrian Pine—The Gigantic, or Lambert's, Pine—The Heavy-wooded Pine--The Lofty or Bhotan Pine—Long-leaved Indian Pine—Dwarf Pines—The Pineaster—The Larch—Prices of Seedling Larches—Diseases of the Larch—Venice Turpentine—The Larch Creating Herbage—The Cedar—The Indian Cedar—The Silver Fir—The Common Silver Fir—Strasburg Turpentine—Balm of Gilead Silver Fir—Canadian Balsam, or Balm of Gilead—Spruce Firs—The Norway Spruce—Douglas's Spruce Fir—The Black Spruce Fir—The Hemlock Spruce Fir—White American Spruce—Miscellaneous Spruce Trees.

Under this heading is comprised one of the most profitable departments of arboriculture, by which land of poor quality in exposed situations, though scarcely of any value when otherwise made use of, can be made to become very productive and remunerative by appropriate tree-planting.

The cone-bearing or resinous species of trees are those best suited for high altitudes, the leading varieties being Scotch pine, pineaster, larch, cedar, silver fir, and spruce. Of these, in the relative order of value, the Scotch fir and the larch are reckoned the highest, after which comes the spruce, followed by the silver fir, pineaster, and cedar. There is no need to mention the various uses to which pine-wood is applied, for where is not fir-timber used? In some respects the larch is more valuable than the Scotch pine, owing to the quicker returns which may be ensured by the former; for whereas, in the case of the Scotch pine, about eighty years are required to bring it into full perfection, the larch may be used as timber at half that age, which results from the fact that the latter, even when quite young, has little or no sapwood, while the other in its youth, is chiefly composed of it.

The wood of the spruce is inferior to that of either the Scotch pine or the larch, but it is useful for scaffolding poles, planks for packing cases, and inferior purposes, and is very useful on the farm in the shape of faggot-wood, or for fence work; in which form it is more durable than the other kind, the young branches being considerably tougher than the others, and consequently more lasting.

The timber of the silver fir is also used for inferior purposes, sometimes as flooring, while the cedar is comparatively seldom resorted to, not being grown on a very extensive scale in this kingdom, and being considered too soft for the ordinary use of the carpenter. Grown, however, under the same conditions as the ancient trees, which were formerly used for doors in Greek and Roman temples, the wood instead of being soft and spongy was amongst the hardest and most durable; and the reasons which have caused this result to take place we shall instance when describing the growth of the cedar tree; the alteration being due to the changed methods of cultivation which now prevail, and the ideas which are held in connection with it, being treated more as an exotic, and an ornamental tree, to stand in rich bottoms, rather than one suitable for a craggy, mountainous range of the highest attitude, to which by nature it is most adapted.

As living objects of great beauty, the trees we have named, being mostly evergreen, are admirably adapted for the improvement and ornamentation of otherwise desolate tracts of country, and they can also be fulfilling another very important object in extending districts capable of sustaining the broad-leaved varieties of trees, which could not be maintained during the early periods of their growth without that shelter which it is in their power to bestow.

Established trees in such situations have the effect of mitigating the natural severity of the climate, and are thus the means of allowing corn and other crops to be raised, by which the quality of the grain is improved, and earlier harvests insured. They also play a very important part in affording shelter to live stock, which is very generally acknowledged by those who have had experience on this head; and while the Scotch pine at its full age rises in grand proportions, the thinnings of the plantation furnish a considerable amount of useful wood, suitable for various purposes while young. The lively, grassy green of the larch in spring time, with its delicate, pinkish catkins, makes a handsome contrast to the sombre scene around; while the spruce and the silver fir are elegant and symmetrical in their proportions, well adapted for the adornment of craggy eminences, with which the grand and striking outline of the cedar ought to be much more frequently associated than it is.

54. **THE PINE TREE.**—The genus *Pinus* embraces a large variety of evergreen trees, which are indigenous to Europe, Asia, and America, their distinguishing features consisting in the arrangement of their leaves, which are needle-shaped, or pointed, arranged in groups of two, three, or five, which are enclosed in a scaly sheath at their

base, most of them producing timber of great size abounding in resin, the resinous products forming no inconsiderable item of commerce.

The spruce produces Burgundy pitch and the best yellow resin; while from the Scotch pine and pinaster, tar, pitch, and lamp-black are furnished. From the silver fir Strasburg turpentine is extracted, while Venice turpentine comes from the larch, which is used very much in veterinary practice for the treatment of bruises, old wounds, and ulcers.

Growing naturally in their native countries they are usually found in large masses, and the course of nature is imitated by the tree planter in the practice which usually prevails in respect to their disposal in Great Britain. The genus usually flowers in May and June, the male and female plants being separate on the same tree, the cones which contain their seed generally becoming ripe in the end of the second year, or about eighteen months from their time of flowering.

PINE TREE.

55. **THE SCOTCH PINE** (*P. sylvestris*).—The Scotch pine is indigenous in the Highlands of Scotland, and also abounds in a wild state in the northern countries of Europe, being invariably found in a healthy soil, being averse to any grassy kind of vegetation, or close herbage of any soil excepting heath. In moor land, the seeds readily come into contact with the ground and vegetate, the stems of the heath forming a protection to the young plants, and yet is open enough to allow them to grow without suffering from confinement.

It is said that in the case of many fir forests the timber has degenerated very much in quality, owing to the fact of the tree having been cultivated for many generations, the seeds having been obtained from trees of an inferior quality. At a low altitude, uncongenial for the best development of the tree, a more abundant supply of cones is obtained, and also at a much earlier age than those grown in the Highlands, and the greater facility for obtaining these cones has resulted in the propagation of trees of an inferior quality.

The belief in this view of the case was deemed to be so correct that the Highland Society of Scotland, in the first quarter of the present century, having the fact of the common degeneracy of the tree brought to its notice, with a view of improving the timber of the country, offered prizes for collecting the greatest quantities of the best seed of the Scotch pine, either sown or sold for sowing, as well as for raising the greatest number of plants, the offers made by the society extending over a period of ten years. A reform was thus effected in the cultivation of the tree, and wide-spread notice directed to the subject, so that planters now raise plants from seed which has been taken direct from the indigenous forests of Scotland; many of the large landed proprietors there, as the Duke of Sutherland and others, having each formed forests consisting of several millions of the plant; and smaller plantations varying in size have been established during the present century in every county in England.

Sir Thomas Dick Lauder, in his edition of "Gilpin's Forest Scenery," gives the following advice respecting the planting of the Scotch pine:—"It should be carefully remembered by planters that sundry wretched and worthless varieties of the Scotch fir have crept into use, which, in some measure, accounts for the miserable appearance of the low-country planted trees. The greatest care should be taken to plant nothing but those trees raised from the seed of the true *Pinus sylvestris* of the mountains."

This natural law of deterioration appears to be now much better understood than formerly, the variation in the quality of the trees having been pointed out by several writers of practical experience during the present and latter half of the last century; the difference existing first having been put on record by the Earl of Haddington, who published a "Treatise on Forest Trees" in 1760.

Loudon also refers to the same subject in the "Arboretum Britannicum," as follows:—"The reason why we wish to keep every variety and sub-variety as distinct as possible is that in the practice of arboriculture, whether for useful or ornamental purposes, a variety is often of as much importance as a species, and sometimes indeed more so; for example, in *P. sylvestris*, the Highland variety is known and acknowledged to produce timber of a superior quality to the common kind."

The cones of the Scotch fir are ripe at the end of the year, and a good deal of trouble often has to be taken in extracting the seeds, which are heated over a kiln that must not advance beyond 130° Fahrenheit, the kiln being laid with deal: brick or metal kilns being unsuitable for drying seeds; but if only a few pounds are required, these may be conveniently extracted by exposure to the sunshine. The seeds or the plants themselves can, however, be bought so cheaply that it is not worth while of anyone, except those who are about to plant upon a very large scale, to take the trouble of extracting the seeds from the cones.

56. **PRICES OF SCOTCH-PINE PLANTS.**—Two years' seedling native Highland pines can be bought for eighteenpence to two shillings per thousand; and those which have been transplanted for one year, at a year old, from two shillings and sixpence to three shillings. Two year seedlings, one year transplanted, five to six shillings per thousand; and two-year-old seedlings, which have stood for two years afterwards in nursery lines, ten to twelve shillings per thousand, the inferior varieties being sold at about the rate of one-third under these quotations.

When raised from seed, the usual time for sowing in England is about the middle of April, but somewhat later in Scotland, the end of April or the first week in May being considered the most appropriate season. Beds should be prepared of the usual width, by being well dug and smoothly raked, and divided by alleys of fifteen inches in width between them. A dry, well pulverised soil is the best to raise seedling pines in, one which will not cake on the top and make a hard surface through which the young plant would have a difficulty in emerging, owing to the combined effects of rain and sunshine.

One pound of good seed is enough to sow a bed twelve yards in length. The surface of the beds should be raked into the alleys, and the seed placed at a depth in accordance with the nature of the soil, which, raked back on to the beds from the alleys, should be used as a cover varying from a quarter to half an inch; the thinner cover being sufficient where the soil is somewhat heavy; but no exact depth can be prescribed, which must depend, to a certain extent, upon the weather; for a depth that would be necessary during the continuance of a long drought would be too great during the prevalence of a rainy season.

The seed-beds are very attractive to birds, which commit serious depredations upon them; foremost amongst which are linnets, pigeons, and partridges; the former being the principal offenders. Beyond keeping these off as well as possible, and the ground clear of weeds, no more attention is required during the first two summers.

At two years old, the seedlings are fit for being planted out, more being used at this age than at any other; but should plants be required that will have to contend with rank surface vegetation, or any other description of herbage than heath, they will be required to be transplanted from the seed-bed into nursery lines (which is done sometimes at one, but more commonly at two years of age), eight or ten inches asunder, the plants standing two or three inches from one another in the rows, which will be of sufficient distance for them to stand for one year; but double of that space must be allowed if the plants are to remain in nursery lines for two years, which will bring them to the greatest size and age at which it is customary to remove the Scotch pine for the purpose of forest planting.

57. **SCOTCH PINE SEEDLINGS FOR BARE EXPOSURES.**—In bare and barren exposures, such as a hill-top, experience has shown that the plants most tenacious of life, and best fitted for such a situation, are those which have stood in the seed-bed for one year, and been afterwards transplanted to the nursery lines for one year more.

There is no tree, perhaps, which grows so freely in soils of opposite qualities. and which produces so large an amount of valuable timber, as the Scotch pine. On dry heath-covered moors, on stony or gravelly soils, or among the fissures of rocks, its roots penetrate and find subsistence, and it flourishes upon what appears to be the scantiest resources. Of all soils which make up the sum and substance of waste lands, pure bog is the most unsuitable to its growth. Stagnant water is fatal to the tree; but it will subsist in a very thin substratum of soil above water, where no other tree of a similar species would grow, the soil most congenial to its growth being a mixture of inorganic matter, which builds up timber.

Plantations of Scotch pine soon begin to make a return to their owner. The first thinnings are valuable for many purposes; the next come in for props for coal mines, and various uses, for which there is always a good demand, and in districts where there are no mines for paling, laths, and other uses, until it reaches its matured condition and is fit for planks for flooring, and the numerous purposes to which deal is applied.

Its quality will be very much regulated by the soil and situation upon which the timber is grown, and also by its age.

Where the Scotch pine has stood very thickly, the timber being cleared off, the surface of the ground has been found covered with decayed foliage, sprays, and bark. This exuviæ of old pine trees forbids any young plants of the same genus to spring up, but the birch is often found to rise spontaneously in such situations, nature thus giving a pretty plain hint to the tree-planter who has to deal with districts so circumstanced.

In its infancy the tree rises in a formal shape, especially in woods which have been planted; yet, in its native wilds, it assumes outlines of massive and irregular formation, trees of great circumference showing clean boles upwards of forty feet in height, some of sixty feet in height having a spread of branches of ninety feet, which are to be met with in remnants of the old forests which are yet standing in the Highlands of Perthshire.

58. **THE CORSICAN PINE** (*P. laricio*).—This tree is a very fine specimen, often attaining a height of a hundred and forty feet in the island of Corsica. It was introduced into England about the middle of the eighteenth century, and is indigenous to the south of Europe, and the west and north of Asia. Like the rest of the species, it embraces many varieties, none of which have been extensively cultivated in Britain for the purpose of raising timber, their application being confined to ornamental uses.

It grows rapidly, but does not succeed in the poorest soils, nor does it thrive at great altitudes. Its timber is white and soft, of no great value except for packing-cases, and is used for inferior flooring, but is appreciated for some purposes, on account of its being soft and easily worked, which causes it to be appropriated for cabinet-making and by sculptors.

Both in the Jardin des Plantes, at Paris, and in Kew Gardens there are very lofty specimens of this tree.

59. **BLACK PINE OF AUSTRIA** (*P. L. austriaca*).—A lofty tree in its native country, where it often reaches the height of a hundred feet. It is of robust growth, in soft soils of opposite qualities, and produces strong, resinous timber. It was first imported into this country about fifty years ago, its mode of cultivation being the same as that of the Scotch pine.

As its roots are apt to grow loose and straggling, the best trees are raised from plants which were transplanted as one-year-old seedlings into nursery lines, where they have remained for either one or two years.

60. **THE STONE PINE** (*P. pinea*).—The stone pine is grown in this country only as an ornamental tree, being a native of the south of Europe, China, and similar climates, and is too delicate for cultivation as a timber tree.

It is commonly met with in Italy, as an ornamental landscape tree. Its seeds, larger than those of any other species of European pine, are of a sweet, agreeable taste, and very nutritious, causing them to be collected and sold as an edible fruit. Those of the common sorts are contained in a strong shell; but the variety *P. p. fragilis* has a thin shell, and is cultivated on account of its fruit in Italy. The tree grows best in a dry, sandy soil near to the sea, but it needs a certain amount of protection, without being too much confined.

It is said to have been introduced into England at the commencement of the sixteenth century.

61. **THE WEYMOUTH PINE** (*P. strobus*).—This tree takes its name from Lord Weymouth, who imported it from America in the beginning of the eighteenth century. On the hill-sides extending from Canada to Virginia, it is frequently met with. The state of Vermont is accredited with the production of the largest specimens, it being sometimes found there one hundred and fifty feet high, and from nine to fifteen feet in circumference.

It has a somewhat formal growth, with silky foliage, and is of delicate appearance, easily raised in a rich, soft soil, if planted in masses, or sheltered from the severity of the weather by the protection of other trees. Its timber is white and soft, being known as the white American pine of commerce; it is remarkably clean and free from knots. It is extensively imported into Britain, being usually employed for inner house carpentry purposes, such as mouldings, wainscots, boardings, &c., being soft and easily worked.

It is propagated in the same manner as the Scotch pine, and although the tree, when young, produces very long top shoots in the course of one summer, its annual progress in England, for fifty or sixty years, does not exceed one foot.

62. **THE CAMBRIAN PINE** (*P. cembra*).—The seeds of this tree are edible, and form part of the regular food of the peasantry of Switzerland, in those cantons where it is indigenous, being also a native of the Alps, Siberia, and Italy.

It is an erect tree with a smooth bark, having fine leaves of a green and silvery appearance, retaining its lateral branches down to the ground, and being of a somewhat dwarf habit. Although growing somewhat slowly when young, it advances with rapidity after it has attained a certain age, and is of considerable duration, so far as its longevity has had the opportunity of being tested, having been introduced into England about a century and a quarter, which is not considered a long period in counting the age of trees. The Duke of Argyll has the credit of its introduction.

There are several varieties, all of which are quite hardy; the timber is finely grained and very fragrant.

63. **THE GIGANTIC OR LAMBERT'S PINE** (*P. lambertiana*).—This tree grows to an enormous height and size in North America, specimens having been described which exceeded two hundred feet, with a circumference of trunk of upwards of fifty feet. It was introduced into England by Douglas, in 1827, to whom we are indebted for so many varieties of North American trees. Its cones measure eighteen inches long.

The difficulty of obtaining the seed causes the tree to be somewhat rare and expensive, but it is hardy, and well adapted for the northern districts of Great Britain. Its leaves are of a bright green colour, four inches in length, and five in a sheath; making shorter yearly shoots than the Weymouth pine, their annual growth seldom exceeding twelve inches; but they become well matured before winter, and are thus able to resist the frost. When only one-year-old seedlings, they sustain without injury the influence of the most severe winters.

The trunk of the full-grown tree is remarkable for its great bulk in proportion to its height, its timber being white, closely grained, and abounding in turpentine. It is described as growing in its native country in districts where the soil appears to consist of sheer sand, and attains its greatest size, and perfects its fruit most abundantly, in situations where one would imagine the land to be quite incapable of supporting such a huge mass of vegetation; the trunk being unusually straight and destitute of branches to about two-thirds of its height.

64. **THE HEAVY-WOODED PINE** (*P. ponderosa*).—This tree is of a remarkably vigorous habit of growth, producing leading shoots which measure an inch in diameter when it is a few years old, and two feet in length; its leaves are thickly set, and from nine to twelve inches long. It was introduced into England in the year 1826, and although otherwise perfectly hardy, is apt to receive injury from the wind.

65. **THE LOFTY OR BHOTAN PINE** (*P. excelsia*).—This tree was introduced into Britain in 1827, being hardy, and also extremely ornamental, its growth being equal to that of the Weymouth pine, to which it bears a strong resemblance, but is stouter and of a more robust growth, its leaves being larger and its habit more drooping. It is a native of the Himalaya mountains, where it ranges from eighty to a hundred feet; the timber being white and resinous, upon the slightest puncture readily yielding a pure and liquid turpentine.

It is produced from imported seed, which grows readily by the ordinary method of propagation.

There are a number of highly ornamental pine trees, as The Long-Leaved Indian Pine (*P. longifolia*), which is perhaps the most beautiful of the species, but too tender to be grown in the open air in Great Britain: *P. gererdiana*, a native of Nepaul, which has seeds nearly an inch long, and are edible; but although the plants will bear the winters of this country, the climate does not seem equal to raising them to the size of a timber tree.

66. **DWARF PINES** (*P. sylvestris pumilio; P. s. mugho; P. s. uncinato*).—Three species of dwarf pines which bear a strong resemblance to the Scotch pine, and are found in cold and exposed situations in mountainous regions, as the Alps and Pyrenees, where they are only bushy shrubs, but attain the size of bushy trees when shelter is given to them. Their foliage is thickly set, of a dark green colour, their habit being broad and spreading, which causes them to be well adapted for cold and windy situations. They all furnish hard, red wood of a durable kind, which is of a very inflammable nature, sufficiently so to be used as torches by the inhabitants of the districts where they are indigenous. They have been cultivated merely as a variety for ornamental purposes, but by repeated propagation they lose to a considerable degree their dwarf proportions, and grow to resemble very much the Scotch pine, which has caused it to be considered that they owe their peculiarities to climate and situation, which has dwarfed their proportions in the course of successive generations, and stunted a growth which would be considerably greater under less trying conditions.

There are a great number of American pines, that continent being the most productive of any for them, yielding the finest coniferæ in the world, as *Pungens*, *Banksiana*, *Rigida*, and *Resinosa*. *P. sabiniana*, a native of the north-west of America, though one of the smallest of the genus here, is said in its native country to reach a height of one hundred feet.

67. **THE PINEASTER, OR CLUSTER PINE.**—This tree was introduced into England at the close of the sixteenth century, and is a most valuable tree for planting in sandy soils by the sea-shore, a deep, dry, sandy soil being indispensable to its profitable growth. It has been the means of reclaiming loose, shifting sands, upon which, at one time, no one would ever have expected to see anything grow in the shape of a timber tree; 12,500 acres of downs in France having been converted into thriving plantations, which were at one time entirely destitute of the slightest particle of vegetation, and which at one time offered to the view only a monotonous repetition of dreary sandy wastes.

The same has also been done in the county of Norfolk, besides other places, and sea-side planting has lately become a subject of great importance to many who possess unprofitable land on the seacoast.

The pineaster does not thrive in a rich, or a wet soil, where it will not endure the frosts of winter; but it has been very successfully grown in poor, sandy soil, where few other species would become timber. It is indigenous to the south of Europe, and those countries which border the Mediterranean, as well as in other parts of the world, having been introduced into England by Gerrard; some of the best specimens which have been planted during the past century and a half being seventy-five feet high and four feet in diameter, which have been grown in pure sand.

In open sand it strikes its roots to a great depth, and finds its sustenance at a long distance below the surface. It generally assumes a pyramidal form, reaching the height of twenty feet in thirty years, but often growing a couple of feet in a summer. All the varieties of this tree are distinguished by their bright green foliage and clustering habit of growth, the bare spaces on the branches from whence the male catkins have been produced, giving to the foliage a singular tufted appearance, its cones being generally produced in groups of a star-like form, from whence the name of pineaster, or star-pine.

The plants are raised both from native and imported seed, and are treated in the same manner as that adopted with the Scotch pine, being covered with soil to the depth of half an inch. At one year of age the seedlings should be put into nursery lines, and as the tree will not bear transplantation, after it has become bare in its roots, it should be either removed early to its final destination or be transplanted frequently in the nursery.

One of the best varieties of the tree, *P. p. escarenus*, was introduced into this country by the Earl of Aberdeen in 1825, from the south of France. *P. p. foliis variegatis* is a very ornamental tree, which is propagated by inarching on any of the common species, but, as we have said before, it is in the character of a sea-side tree that the pineaster possesses such remarkable value.

68. **THE LARCH.**—This is the only deciduous tree of the coniferous order, or cone-bearing tribe, and was introduced into England during the early part of the seventeenth century, although mentioned much earlier by Gerrard, to whom we have before referred, who in 1596 published a list of trees comprising those both of native and foreign growth; the first account of its having become naturalised in this country being given by Parkinson, a London apothecary, who wrote about the year 1629.

For a long time, however, in England, the tree maintained but a very subsidiary position, its nature not being properly understood. Nurserymen, to their astonishment, found out at last that those trees which had been planted in the worst situations had thriven the best; and from this time a more correct appreciation of its requirements became known, these being an elevated open sub-soil, from which moisture is rapidly discharged, situated in a clear and open atmosphere.

The larch was thus established a hundred years in England before its introduction into Scotland, the fertile plains of the first-named portion of the kingdom not being nearly so appropriate for its growth as the hilly ranges of the latter; most of the large trees which are found in England standing in the vicinity of high hills and running streams.

According to an account of the "Transactions of the Highland Society," the first larches were said to have been planted by the Duke of Atholl's trustees, some plants having been brought down from London by Mr. Menzies, of Migeny. five of which were left at Dunkeld, and eleven at Blair, in Athole, those at Dunkeld being planted on the lawn, in alluvial, gravelly soil, in a sheltered situation, forty feet above the Tay and a hundred and thirty above the sea-level.

From 1730 to 1740 the larch was planted by several of the Scottish landowners, but they were mostly treated improperly, being inserted either into soil too rich for them, or too near the residences of the proprietors, where the tree had not space enough to develop itself; and at first it did not attract that share of attention which it was ultimately destined to do, and prove such a valuable addition to our catalogue of timber trees, performing most important offices in the economical and profitable management of land.

LARCH.

The larch grows quickly when young, much more so than any other coniferous tree, and is consequently of great value in extirpating furze and rank herbage. With this object in view two year transplanted plants are used, and placed in the position they are destined to occupy immediately after the furze has been cut down. Planted three or four feet from one another, they get the start of the furze, which they will overtop and suffocate; and thus do away with the necessity of frequent clearings of the ground in order to encourage the growth of the trees; an operation which is attended with a certain amount of expense. As soon as the herbage is subdued, the larches require early and gradual thinning.

When the heath is short, good one-year-old seedling larches, which will sometimes be from six to eight inches high, are adapted for being permanently planted out in moor-land, where the soil is favourable; but two-year-old plants are the most frequently employed, their average height being from twelve to fifteen inches, which reach above short herbage.

Both on account of economy as well as appearance, the larch is invariably associated with some other tree, larches standing by themselves presenting a bare and uninteresting appearance during a considerable portion of the year, and it thrives better in a mixed plantation, liking especially the fellowship of the Scotch pine, but yet better still the companionship of the oak, which derives its sustenance from a great depth of soil, and does not so much interfere with its food supplies; while the late development of the foliage of the oak causes it not to overshadow the larch, which is thus brought into leaf early in the season from the amount of exposure it obtains.

The distances at which larches and other trees should be placed in a plantation will depend a good deal upon circumstances, and must be regulated by the situation. Bleak and exposed moorlands in Scotland usually have assigned to them 4,000 plants per acre. But on low, sheltered situations, 3,000 are generally found sufficient, the proportion of larch plants being usually from a fourth to a half of the number employed, which is made again to depend upon the suitableness of the land for the growth of the tree, and the value of the thinnings, which vary very much in different neighbourhoods.

By planting the different trees at uniform intervals, a choice will be afforded in thinning the plantation, so that the trees may stand alternately, or be made to consist of one species only, if so desired.

The larch will flourish in soils of very opposite qualities, being found growing in dry and sandy, as well as wet and clayey ones, fine specimens being met with in exceedingly varied situations; but it grows to the best advantage on the slopes and rugged formations of the soil—as, for example, when a landslip has occurred.

Where stagnant water accumulates, it speedily becomes diseased; and liking a cool and elevated situation, in low positions, sufficient space should be allowed to it for the full development of its foliage. In many of the Highland districts of Scotland, the mountain sides may be seen clothed with larch trees associated with the Scotch pine, no other tree, perhaps, having been so generally adopted in so short a space of time as the larch, from the time of its introduction into the sister kingdom.

Opinion is not unanimous as to the relative production of timber of the larch and Scotch pine respectively, when produced at great altitudes. The failure of the larch to become large-sized trees, in some of these situations, has been accounted for in the fact that not unfrequently the surface soils at great altitudes are composed of too pure a peat, which is less adapted to the larch than to the growth of the native tree.

No amount of cold seems to have any effect upon it during the winter, when its branches are bare, but few trees are more keenly sensitive to frost when out in foliage, its fine and tender leaves being immediately affected by change of weather. On sunny slopes in a fine season, when the end of March and the beginning of April brings the trees into leaf, they often receive a considerable amount of injury by the late frosts, which they are always slow to recover from, and are, indeed, occasionally killed by, this having happened in some instances to large plantations on southern slopes, a few years after the young trees were planted, while the more backward ones on northern declivities escaped.

The common larch is the only tree of the genus that is worth cultivation on account of its timber, all the other species being comparatively worthless for this purpose, however interesting they may be as specimens in collections. Some of the varieties yield red and some white blossoms, or female catkins, while others have a delicate pink blossom, and all intermediate shades between red and white. The young wood of the trees and the ripe cones exhibit the same tints of colour, so that the various kinds may be recognized in the absence of blossoms, the red appearing to be the hardiest tree, and best adapted to a late climate.

The larch blossoms and ripens its cones in the same year, which takes place in the beginning of winter, and when cones are collected for seed they should be carefully chosen, the largest cones being the best, the plants rising large or small according to the size of the seeds when collected from healthy trees or otherwise. As, however, the plants can be bought so cheaply, it is scarcely worth while to raise them from seed, unless very large quantities are wanted, or individuals prefer to make the experiment.

69. **PRICES OF SEEDLING LARCHES.**—The rates at which young trees sell is much as follows:—One-year-old seedlings, 2*s.* per thousand; two year, 3*s.* to 4*s*; one year transplanted, 6*s.* to 7*s.*; two year, 10*s.* to 12*s.*: the price of seed being generally about 15*s.* to 21*s.* per pound, while boreing and cutting up the cones is a troublesome operation, though of course simplified very much by those who make a business of preparing the seed.

In raising plants from seed, sowing should be performed about the middle of April, in the southern counties of England; and in the north of the kingdom, the last week of that month. If the ground is poor, old, well rotted manure, decayed leaves, or vegetable mould, should be used, but it is best to let them follow a crop for which the land has been previously well manured. Beds should be formed as usual, four feet in width, in light, well pulverized soil, and smoothly raked over.

One pound of seed is enough to sow a seed-bed of the dimensions of four lineal yards, and they should be covered to the depth of a quarter of an inch of soil. In a fortnight or three weeks, according to the weather, the plants will make their appearance, and the beds must be protected against the depredations of birds. As they are also visited by the grub-worm, situations should be chosen which are not subject to its ravages. The beds should be kept clear of weeds throughout the season.

By the end of September the young plants will have completed their first year's growth, when they should stand pretty thickly upon the ground, and be from four to seven inches in height. The soil should be loosened with a fork, and half of the number of plants standing in the seed-bed thinned out during the following winter or spring, and transplanted into nursery lines about fifteen inches asunder, the plants standing in the rows a few inches from each other. They should be allowed to stand thus for a year, when they will be ready to be planted out with the others which were undisturbed, which will then have become two-year-old seedlings. They should never be allowed to remain standing more than two years undisturbed in the seed-bed.

But if stout plants are required, as we have before described, they should be allowed to remain for two years in the nursery lines. Nurserymen make a practice of removing every other line in the bed of one-year-old transplanted plants, which gives the remaining lines which are to stand two years a distance of two feet and a half asunder.

At two years of age the plants generally are two to two feet and a half high, which is of sufficient age and stature to permit of their being planted in the roughest forest ground. When two-year-old seedlings are put into nursery lines and allowed to stand there for two years, they mostly reach the height of three feet, which is the extreme limit of age the young trees are used for transplantation.

The larch, in a congenial soil and under proper treatment, is said to produce more timber than any other tree; a common fault in its management being the neglect of early thinning, it being, perhaps, the tree most readily injured from want of sufficient space to grow in. It is said by experienced persons in the management of larch plantations, that the common error of not allowing them sufficient space at a critical period of their existence—just when they begin to attain the size of a timber tree, say, from ten to twenty years of age—is productive of great loss to the owner; for, on account of their leaves being tender and minute, they present only a small surface to the influence and operation of the atmosphere, so that on a level surface, in a plantation composed of trees of the same size, the leaves fail to elaborate the sap absolutely necessary for the formation of timber, and the trunks become bare, stunted, and bark-bound.

On unequal surfaces, as upon hill-sides, more space is obtained for its foliage to be exposed to the light. At the same time, close planting is necessary in rearing larch timber in bleak and exposed situations, to prevent the play of biting winds upon the surface of the ground, at seasons when the tree is most likely to suffer at the opening of the season; for although the top is necessarily the least sheltered, it needs it the least, inasmuch as the leaves of a healthy young plant are always first expanded near the ground, and some time before the top ones are exposed to the influence of the weather—the top bud being developed at a later time, when there is not so much need for protection.

In close planting, too, the result of a thick cover is, that with their united branches and foliage in almost direct contact with the ground, the native herbage becomes smothered and destroyed, and the decayed stems and roots are converted into manure, which goes a long way towards the support of the growing trees, which is proved by the progress a plantation makes immediately after the trees have formed a cover, and so suppressed the surface vegetation. Although broad-leaved trees, which have been neglected in their infancy, may, by subsequent good management, be restored to health and a proper figure, there is no doing this in the larch when it has been stunted by confinement and reduced to a scanty supply of foliage.

70. **DISEASES OF THE LARCH.**—The larch is somewhat liable to various casualties, more especially when planted in low situations, and when not mixed with other trees.

The insect called *Coccus laricis* rarely visits trees of vigorous growth which stand at a high altitude in company with others; but in confined woods, in a humid atmosphere, it very often prevails to a serious extent, especially in wet seasons. After late frosts in spring its effects are the worst, and trees which are visited by these insects never advance much in growth, their sap appearing to escape from them out of numerous perforations, which cover them with a dusky coating, somewhat resembling in appearance the effects produced by smoke. The least injurious results are experienced when there is a free circulation of the atmosphere, and also when the plantation is not composed entirely of larches. There appears to be no cure, beyond taking advantage of every method for securing the health of the plantation which can be adopted.

The larch is also subject to the visitation of atmospheric blight, which happens at different times of the season when the tree is in full leaf, but most commonly about the end of July or beginning of August, blasting the foliage, and giving to it the appearance of premature ripening, especially the oldest leaves, the most recently expanded not suffering to so great an extent, save in exceptional cases.

These results are often attributed to frost when they must be set down to the kind of blight we have described, the effect of which will be made apparent during the ensuing summer by a want of foliage, and the presence of numerous dead twigs throughout the trees.

A disease, literally the rot, but which goes by the name of "pumping" in some districts, from the similarity its effects produce upon the tree to the appearance its hollow trunk bears to a wooden pipe, or pump, is often met with in larch plantations.

It is supposed the disease spreads upwards from the roots, but it is not always confined to the centre of the tree, prevailing mostly in ground where other timber has been grown before, the decaying roots and the fungus which accompanies them tending to injure the roots of many kinds of trees, of which the larch appears to be the most sensitive.

Manure of any kind is injurious to the larch, and the common plan resorted to in pit-planting, of putting the top sward, or turf, into the bottom of the pit, to rot there, is unfavourable to the larch, and is a practice which ought not to be followed; and as we have mentioned before, young plants are always to be preferred. On a retentive soil, where the surface moisture is not carried off, the roots of the larch are apt to suffer, and its weakest fibres to rot, from excessive moisture.

Another cause is also attributed, the strain of the wind acting upon its roots. The shape of the larch naturally, admirably adapts it for being supported by a small root; but when the necessary thinning has not been carried out in a plantation, the proper proportions of the tree become destroyed by confinement, so that, possessing top branches only, they seldom escape the influence of the wind, which subjects their roots to a strain, by which they suffer injury, which is followed by decay.

The effect of the wind may be very plainly seen upon a close plantation, and like some other surface-rooting trees, such as poplars and different kinds of elms, the larch has a tendency to get disease in its trunk, and therefore requires a little more attention than ordinary, so as to preserve it in a sound state, the causes we have mentioned inducing decay of the trunk.

In certain districts, where rot has prevailed extensively, many landowners have refrained from planting the larch, while in others no case of disease has occurred. In some instances the decay commences at the top, the roots being perfectly sound; which shows there exists a certain amount of susceptibility in it to rot, especially in ill-drained, low-lying districts, though in the dryest bottoms it is not always exempt, exposed situations, such as the sides of mountains, where the water from above flows off the surface of the soil, suiting it the best.

In low situations a northern aspect is the most favourable to the growth of the larch, owing to the smaller liability of the buds suffering from the late frosts, which injure those which are stimulated by warm southern exposures, and when in its full vigour the tree is better qualified to resist disease, as may naturally be supposed to be the case. By early and repeated thinning, so that complete and unimpeded exposure of the entire foliage to light and air is secured, some of the evils we have mentioned will be averted. Without a proper circulation of air, and exposure to sunshine, the juices of the sap will not be properly elaborated, and this must be done, it must be remembered, through the instrumentality of the leaves, which being very small, present only a minute surface to the action of the elements.

The same principle is at work here as that we have deprecated before, in the case of men who are in the habit of stripping off nearly all the side branches of trees, in the belief they were encouraging the growth of the trunk, when indeed they were cutting off some of its supplies.

Judicious lopping is sometimes necessary, but injudicious treatment in this respect is much more common.

Canker also visits the tree occasionally, which is generally found to make its appearance in wet situations, and sometimes upon a site where corn has previously been grown. The tree decays in various places, and a black substance issues from the affected part, and its entire growth becomes irregular. There would seem to be no cure for this, except to avoid establishing trees in doubtful places.

Larch is not in itself particularly subject to fungi, though it suffers from contamination from that of other trees. This must be borne in mind upon those occasions when it is made to follow the Scotch pine, the trees often becoming unsound; so that disadvantages, as well as advantages, must be balanced against one another, the result arising from the well-known principle of gangrenous matter communicating disease to that it comes into contact with, happening in those cases where the dead roots of the fir touch those of the living larch.

For agricultural purposes, larch wood in its various stages of growth is extremely useful. It is very durable as posts in building, for paling, hop-poles, and for all purposes where wood comes into contact with the ground, which causes it to be very appropriate for railway sleepers, &c. Having a tendency to warp, it is more seldom employed than other deal for such purposes as flooring, &c., though well adapted for rafters, joists, and similar uses.

Its bark is sometimes used for tanning, though it only fetches half the price that is obtained for oak bark; but its bulk being twice that of oak, in proportion to its weight, it is seldom manufactured profitably.

71. **VENICE TURPENTINE.**—A healthy larch tree when tapped

is said to yield seven or eight pounds of Venice turpentine yearly for forty or fifty years, the turpentine flowing from May to September In order to procure it, the full-grown tree in its native districts is pierced to the centre with an auger. The turpentine is made to flow into a trough through a tube, and no further preparation is required beyond straining the liquor so obtained through a coarse hair cloth. The timber is, however, spoilt by the operation.

CEDAR.

72. **THE LARCH CREATING HERBAGE.**—Perhaps, however, one of the most valuable properties of the larch is its power for producing herbage, which is made to grow by the fertilising effects of its rich foliage, which it sheds annually. In a healthy plantation the deposit is very considerable; the leaves dropping down and becoming incorporated with the soil where they fall. On sandy sites, where larch has been felled, the surface has become clothed with some of the finest natural grasses, and good pasture land has thus been obtained, the roots of the trees being comparatively easily moved.

73. **THE CEDAR** (*Abies cedrus*, or *Cedrus libani*).—The cedars of

Lebanon, which have been extolled by the Hebrew prophets in sacred history, is an evergreen tree indigenous to Mount Lebanon in Syria and to Mount Atlas in the north of Africa; being the most imposing and magnificent of all the cone-bearing trees, remarkable more for the size of its trunk and its enormous expansion of branches than its height. From the knowledge which practical men have of the wood of the cedar yielded by trees in this country, which is of a very soft nature, they imagine that the cypress or some other tree must have furnished the timber of biblical times; but it can be pretty clearly proved that the quality of the timber has very much degenerated, by being propagated both in an unsuitable climate and an unfavourable position for the best development of the quality of its timber.

If we take the instance of Lebanon, its summit is nearly 10,000 feet high, parts of the loftiest peaks being covered with snow all the year round. The trees not standing on the top of the mountain, but in the valley, and the elevated site they occupy, which is affected by the melting snow above them, is peculiarly adapted for the natural habit of the tree, and for the bringing out of its best qualities. The nature of the tree still remains unaltered, and modern experience shows us that similar positions are best adapted for the tree. Instead of being grown in appropriate situations in Britain, on the sides of craggy precipices, and others, suited for the tribe of coniferæ to which it belongs, like the Highland Scotch pine, it is more often planted as an ornamental tree in rich, low-lying ground, where its growth is unnaturally stimulated, and its timber necessarily becomes deteriorated in consequence of its propagation in both an unsuitable soil and situation.

The celebrated trees of Lebanon have been described by many travellers, there being only a few remaining of the very ancient ones, said to have been planted by Solomon in the quincunx order in which they now stand, and for which the Arabs of all sects entertain a traditional veneration; a grove of younger cedars being around the ancient patriarchs, which remain standing, all of them being much furrowed by lightning.

The cedar seldom produces cones before it is forty years old, and sometimes not before it reaches a hundred years, and the seeds cannot be depended upon to vegetate until several crops of cones have been produced. The catkins appear in autumn, and the cones require two years to attain maturity, but do not drop, nor discharge their seed like other coniferous trees under the influence of sunshine, but remain attached to the tree for many years unless the cones are gathered. This should be done before the beginning of April, and the seeds extracted, which is a most difficult operation with fresh cones. Seeds are imported from the Levant, and those grown upon English trees are also used in this country.

To raise plants from seed, it should be sown in April, in light friable ground, standing about an inch asunder, and be covered with about half an inch depth of soil. The young plants generally break through the ground in about six weeks after planting, when the advantage of close sowing will be made apparent from the comparative ease with which they emerge from the ground. In the case of their sowing when the surface of the ground gets only slightly crusted over, or caked by alternate rain and sunshine, the weak plants are unable to force themselves through.

In nurseries, the seed is sometimes sown in heat under glass, and the young plants are potted off in June when their seed-leaves are only full grown. Another practice is to remove the plants when they are a year old into small pots, and change them into larger ones as they increase in size. This method suits nurserymen very well, as they can always insure their safe removal, and can dispose of them at any time of the year as their customers may want them; but if required by thousands, this method is attended with a great deal of trouble and expense; and to render this unnecessary when large numbers are wanted, the plan of transplanting the seedling plants at the age of one or two years into nursery lines should always be adopted, until they are removed to their final destination; for if allowed to remain longer, the roots of the cedar, like the rest of the coniferæ we have described, are apt to take a wide range and lose the bushiness of root which is indispensable for their successful removal.

The comparative slow growth of the cedar is undoubtedly the main cause why its cultivation is not more extensively followed than it is, but its slow growth when young is often due to the plants being stunted in their early progress, through not being transplanted in the way recommended; and it undoubtedly deserves to be much more extensively resorted to as a timber tree than now obtains.

The situations which are favourable to the growth of the Scotch pine are also the best adapted to the cedar, provided the soil is sufficiently good, and where the influence of streams from neighbouring eminences may fertilise their roots.

The prophet Ezekiel speaks of this inclination of the tree when referring to it:—"Thus was he fair in his greatness, in the length of his branches, for his roots were by great waters"; and some large trees at Chelsea became decayed when a pond was removed, from which their roots had doubtless derived sustenance. A rich loam, or sandy clay soil, is one very suitable for the cedar, with an open subsoil, sufficiently above the rise of water, but near enough for the extremities of the roots to have access to it.

74. **THE INDIAN CEDAR** (*C. deodara*).—This tree was introduced into Britain in 1822, and was found to succeed very well, being quite hardy. It is a native of India, attaining a height of

one hundred and fifty feet, with a trunk ten feet in diameter, being found in Nepaul, Cashmere, and Kamaou, at elevations ranging from 7,000 to 12,000 feet above the level of the sea. It is accounted sacred by the Hindoos, and is commonly found in the neighbourhood of their ancient temples.

It bears a strong resemblance to the cedar of Lebanon, but it grows more freely, with a pendulous spray, and is admirably adapted for a lawn tree; but its beauty as a young plant often causes it to be inserted in situations which are destitute of sufficient space for its full development, so that it cannot rise in the full grandeur which is natural to it in a favourable position.

Plants have been known to grow at a rate of twenty inches to two feet annually, its cones being of the size and shape of those of the cedar of Lebanon, but they are deciduous, and fall to scales immediately upon becoming ripe in October or November. A plant at sixteen years of age is recorded to have reached 17 feet in height, its trunk measuring 2 feet 9 inches in circumference.

The seeds should be sown in the April following the October in which they became ripe, and the mode of rearing them is the same as that recommended for the cedar of Lebanon. The seeds, however, lose their vitality if kept beyond seven or eight months.

Plants are sometimes propagated by cuttings, by grafting, and by inarching upon the larch; but seedlings are far better than either.

The timber of the *Deodara* is compact and resinous, emitting a pleasant odour, and takes a high polish. It has been found perfectly sound in the roofs of temples which have been known to have stood for upwards of two hundred years; and it agrees exactly in its nature with that of the cedar-wood which has been described as the product of Syria in biblical and other records, but it has never been found in the Holy Land.

On account of its comparative scarceness, in wholesale quantities, the plants fetch a high price, forty to fifty pounds per thousand being charged for them, and fancy rates are obtained for individual specimens.

75. **THE SILVER FIR.**—This genus, that of *Picea* of Linnæus, is one of the most ornamental trees of the coniferous order, and embraces several species which are indigenous to the continents of Europe, Asia, America, and the north of Africa. It bears a striking resemblance to the spruce fir, from which it differs in the leaves being less numerous and lying more flat on both sides of the branches, which thus form two ranks, while the cones stand erect

on them, and, when ripe, fall away, being deciduous, while those of the spruce fir are pendant and their scales persistent. There are some very beautiful trees amongst the various species, all of which advance in an uniform manner of growth, with a straight trunk tapering regularly, large in proportion to the lateral branches, which range horizontally, and present a flat surface of foliage.

76. **THE COMMON SILVER FIR** (*Picea pectinata*).—In the narrow valleys in the south of Germany, between the Swiss mountains and the Black Forest, on rich, friable, loamy soils, this tree attains a height of one hundred and fifty feet, with a trunk from five to six and a half feet in diameter. It is also indigenous in the north of Africa, and on the lower slopes of the mountains and in the glens of France, Italy, Spain, and Germany, and was introduced into England about the year 1603, by Serjeant Newdigate, two trees which he planted at Harefield Park, Middlesex, being described by Evelyn, in 1679, as having become "goodly masts," one being eighty-one feet in height and thirteen feet in circumference, the other being of smaller dimensions, on account of its having been scorched on one side, from the burning of the house adjoining the place where it stood.

When young the silver fir is one of the most tender trees which is reared in Britain; but although its growth is slow during the first ten or fifteen years of its life, yet, after getting well established in a suitable soil, and attaining a tolerable height, it grows rapidly both in height and girth, and is seldom after this period exceeded in the rate of progress by any other tree of the coniferous order.

It will thrive in soils of very opposite qualities, but the one most suitable for producing fine specimens of trees, is a rich deep loam, which is cool and moist, and not too dry, usually to be met with along the slopes of moorland at not too high an altitude; but it will grow in stiff clay, and in almost any kind of soil that is not too severely affected by prolonged drought. It is unfit for the bare and lofty elevations upon which the Scotch pine and the larch flourish, in the countries where it is indigenous being generally found associated with the oak.

It is a most useful tree for filling up vacancies in woods, and for being planted amidst timber which has soon to be removed, the excess of shelter in such situations, which would be fatal to some kinds of trees, being beneficial to it; promoting its growth by shielding it from the effects of the late frosts which are so likely to injure it in this country during its infancy.

The yearly growth of the silver fir, when young, is always very short, and as the buds of the top shoot are mostly unfolded at the same time as those of the lateral branches, and are exceedingly tender, the plant generally suffers at the first commencement of the season. When, however, it has reached the height of ten or fifteen feet, and has become well established, it shoots vigorously and becomes more robust in its habit, and the buds on the older and lower branches become first developed, while those on the top expand themselves at a later period, when they are generally safe from injury.

The species has been chiefly planted for ornamental effect, and has seldom been reared in masses by itself; but where this has been done in a suitable soil, it has been found that they admit of standing very close together upon the ground, which has the effect of producing tall timber of a fine grain, and, unlike most other trees, which under such conditions would run up with slender trunks, the boles are found to attain a large girth, notwithstanding the unusual closeness of their position, so that the cubical contents of the timber per acre are seldom exceeded by any other tree.

Specimens are found interspersed throughout most of the English counties, which considerably exceed in height that of most other timber trees, ranging from 110 to 150 feet in height. The wood is generally of a pale yellow, and the texture of its grain very irregular, even in different parts of the same tree, if it has reached a large size. When grown into the form of timber, it is commonly used for such purposes as flooring, from the quality it possesses of being free from a tendency to warp; and when raised in masses the timber is more equal and better in quality than that which stands separately.

The seeds become ripe in the beginning of winter, and they should be sown in April, in a well-pulverised soil. The plants should stand in the seed-bed at a distance of an inch and a half from one another; and to insure this result, much will depend upon their average fertility, which varies very much, according to the season, and is indicated by their being full and plump, or the reverse; and the soil should be covered over the seeds at the depth of about half an inch. The young plants generally make their appearance about the end of May, up to which time they should be well protected from the depredations of the birds.

Should the plants come up before May, it is necessary they should be protected, as the slightest touch of frost will destroy them. This can be effectually done by sheltering the beds with a cover of broom or the branches of any evergreen trees, laid lightly upon the surface, or if small boughs are stuck up endwise in the ground, close enough to form a shelter for the young plants, but not so close as to shut out the air.

Some nurserymen, in districts where the late frosts are apt to prove injurious, cover the beds immediately they are sown with straight-drawn straw, and to secure it in its place and to protect the covering from the wind, a straw rope is stretched along the centre of the bed, and is fixed by pegs to the ground.

When the plants are late in making their appearance, they suffer less during the first year, perhaps, than during the later years of their infant course. The young growth and newly expanded foliage is destroyed by the frosts of early May, or late in April, when its influence appears to have been scarcely felt on any other trees, so that twigs of evergreens, or some light covering, is often needed to protect the tops of the young plants.

After standing two years in the seed-bed the plants should be transplanted into nursery lines; but in the event of their having been frost-bitten, it is usual to allow them to remain for the third year, in order to give them an opportunity of forming tops, which they do the more readily from not being disturbed.

In transplanting them into nursery lines, choice should be made of a sheltered situation in preference to one of a sunny exposure, which is more likely to produce healthy and well-topped plants. The lines should be a foot apart, the plants standing in the rows a few inches asunder. After standing in the lines for two summers they should be carefully lifted, and either be planted in those situations where they are intended to stand, or replanted in a wider space in order to allow them to become of a larger size before the final planting out.

The early growth of the plants so treated is so slow that at the age of six years they seldom exceed one foot in height, but their roots are large and bulky in proportion to their size, and the stems are also comparatively stout in proportion to the height of the plant.

77. **STRASBURG TURPENTINE.**—The resinous fluid which is collected from the small tumour-like blisters formed under the outer bark is the Strasburg turpentine of commerce, which takes its name from the extensive produce of the turpentine contiguous to that town. It is the only tree of the tribe that yields turpentine, which is used in the preparation of clear varnishes and artists' colours. The essential oil of turpentine, which is much esteemed for the use made of it in cases of strains and bruises, is the product of the tree, as well as several articles which are resorted to by the veterinary surgeon.

78. **THE BALM OF GILEAD SILVER FIR** (*P. balsamea*).—This is an American tree which was introduced into this country at

the end of the seventeenth century. It is much hardier when young than the common silver fir, yielding its cones abundantly in England, and being readily grown from seed in the same manner as the preceding, but is of much quicker growth, being generally, at five or six years of age, twice the size of the common silver fir, and at the age of eight or ten years, three times its height. This vigour is, however, but of short duration, and it often ceases to grow before it is twenty years of age.

In the best soil adapted for its growth, that which is at once deep, moist, and well sheltered, it seldom lives beyond the age of thirty or forty years, and it is considered a fine specimen of the tree which reaches forty feet in height. Still, it is a useful tree in many respects, both on account of its early and rapid growth as well as for its highly ornamental effect and the shelter it gives to all newly formed plantations in which it is placed, adding considerably to their richness and effect. Its foliage is closely set, being denser and shorter than that of the common silver fir. At the age of ten years it is usually ten or eleven feet high, advancing in its growth in a pyramidal form, affording protection until plants of greater duration become established. In light gravelly soils, where the subsoil becomes affected by the drought of summer, it puts on a sickly aspect, and soon dies; but in a rich soil of ordinary moisture its foliage wears a hue of the darkest green, of the most luxuriant description.

79. **CANADIAN BALSAM, OR BALM OF GILEAD.**—The tree takes its name from the resinous extract it produces, which is known in its native country by the name of Canadian Balsam, or Balm of Gilead; a certain preparation of its turpentine being said to have great efficacy in the treatment of consumption in certain stages of that disorder. This resinous exudation is made more profusely than by any other tree, the bark, buds and cones being often literally smothered in turpentine, which is highly odoriferous, and of the most penetrating taste. Upon the slightest incision being made in the tree, the turpentine flows copiously; and this excessive overflow, without doubt, tends to the early decay of the tree.

Its timber is used for the ordinary purposes to which common deal is applied.

80. **SPRUCE FIRS** (*Abies*).—This genus belongs to *Coniferæ* in the natural order of plants, and to *Monœcia monadelphia* in the Linnæan system, and consists of several species of evergreen trees indigenous to Europe, Asia, and America. They affect a soft and moist soil, associated with a cool climate, and are remarkable for their erect form and profusion of foliage.

81. **THE NORWAY SPRUCE** (*A. excelsa*).—This is a native of Norway, Sweden, the north of Germany, Denmark, and Lapland, being the commonest tree of the genus that is cultivated in Britain, and is generally considered to be the loftiest one indigenous to

Europe, in some of the valleys of its native countries having been known to attain a height of one hundred and eighty feet.

It is a beautiful tree, of very uniform growth, assuming a conical form, retaining even in advanced age its branches and luxuriant foliage down to the surface of the ground. It was introduced into Britain at an early period, and although it is so hardy that it is never affected by any degree of frost during winter, yet it does not attain to a very large size in exposed situations.

It derives its nourishment chiefly from the surface, and prefers a soil which is at once cool and moist. With a surface-soil of ordinary quality, it is one of the few trees which will thrive where the subsoil is wet and retentive; and even in dry and sandy soil, which is unsuitable for the production of spruce timber, it develops itself sufficiently to form an excellent shelter for establishing other trees, which ultimately become more valuable; but after reaching a certain age upon such soils, and nearing its completeness as a timber-tree, it begins to assume a sickly aspect, its foliage becoming thin, and offering a striking contrast to the luxuriousness of its growth under conditions more favourable to its longevity and health—such as it finds in the cool alluvial deposit of the sheltered glen, where it puts on its most attractive shape and features.

It blossoms in England in May and June, and the cones, which are produced abundantly, get ripe in the following winter. The seeds are sown in the same way as those of the Scotch pine, and when the plants have stood for two seasons in the seed-bed, they generally are found to be from seven to nine inches high, and fit for transplantation. In some soils which are unfavourable to them, or in adverse seasons, they are of weaker growth, in which case, if they stand thin in the seed-bed, they may remain another year, and be transplanted after the third summer.

No other species of the *Coniferæ* will allow of this being done so well, but the spruce having naturally fibrous roots, it is better adapted for removal than the others. Sometimes the plants are lifted direct from the seed-beds to the place where they are ultimately destined to stand. This, of course, must mainly depend upon the nature of the land to which it is intended to remove them.

In moor-land, when the surface herbage is not too coarse and strong for plants of this size, they will do very well, particularly when the soil is of a nature favourable to their growth. The usual practice followed is, however, to transplant the seedlings into nursery lines for one or two years, according to the description of the ground in which they are to be placed.

Although one-year transplanted plants are but very little bigger than they were at the time of their removal from the seed-bed, yet the seedlings are considerably stronger and more robust in constitution, their roots being bushier, and they are hardier altogether from the process they have gone through, so that they suffer less when finally planted out. Should it be the intention to remove them after having stood one year only in lines, they can be put into the ground much closer than when the intention is to allow them to remain for two years. With this object in view, the lines need not be more than eight inches apart, and the plants two inches asunder; but if the latter, the lines should be a foot apart, and the plants four inches from one another as they stand in the rows.

Two-year transplanted plants are those usually employed in the formation of plantations, but if they are allowed a sufficient space to stand in they may safely be allowed to remain for three years, when they should be removed either to the forest, or be transplanted again into nursery lines, so as to insure their future vigour. Even though more seldom disturbed the spruce will admit of being removed at a larger size than any other of the coniferous trees during its growth in the nursery.

When established in a suitable soil for a few years, the species will make rapid progress, and between the age of fifteen and thirty years its top shoots two feet in length annually, and when it has moderate shelter it will often reach sixty feet in forty years. The timber is white and soft, and is also finely grained, but it is free from knots only when it is grown in a close plantation. Its value seldom exceeds the price of the most inferior Scotch pine, and it is used for railway sleepers, planks and spars; for small masts, scaffolding poles, boarding for roofing, &c., the resinous production of the tree forming Burgundy pitch, which consists of its congealed sap, melted and clarified by boiling water.

82. **DOUGLAS'S SPRUCE FIR** (*A. douglash*).—This splendid tree, which bears the name of the celebrated Scotch collector, is a native of the banks of the Columbia river, in North-west America, and was first produced in England from seed in 1827. It is a magnificent fast-growing tree, many handsome specimens of which are spread about the country. One of these attained the height of nineteen feet in ten years, when it began to produce cones.

The species is quite hardy, but has not yet had sufficient time to develop itself into an object of national importance. According to the description given of them by Douglas, the trunks of these trees in the forests of North-west America range from two feet to ten feet in diameter, and from one hundred feet to one hundred and eighty feet in height.

Here in England the tree frequently forms leading shoots which will measure three feet long in one season, and yet be of bushy habit in proportion, its foliage being of the richest description, and bearing a strong resemblance to that of a very vigorous yew tree.

LINDEN TREE.

It is believed, like other trees of the spruce variety, to thrive best in soil which has a moist subsoil, which the summer drought does not affect. Instances have occurred where the tree has been planted on gravelly and open subsoil, when it grew very freely at first, but upon a long drought occurring, it died off very suddenly, and the conclusion deduced from this, and similar experience is, that excess of drought is more likely to be injurious to trees of vigorous growth than those whose progress has been slower and more gradual.

Douglas gives the particulars of a stump of this tree which he measured near Fort St. George, on the Columbia river, the dimensions of which, exclusive of the bark, and at three feet from the ground, were forty-eight feet in circumference.

83. **THE BLACK SPRUCE FIR** (*A. nigra*).—This species seldom produces trunks of very large diameter, but it is remarkable for keeping up its ordinary girth when the trees stand unusually close to one another. It is a native of North America, and was introduced into Great Britain at the end of the seventeenth century.

The extreme height it appears to reach is a little over fifty feet, being seldom found of loftier stature even in its native forests in Lower Canada, Nova Scotia, New Brunswick, and the district of Maine, where it is indigenous.

In this country it is grown as an ornamental tree, and not for the sake of its timber, its foliage being rich and dense, and also for its hardness. It likes a moist soil, and gives great shelter and seclusion, for which it is most valued. Its lateral branches, under favourable circumstances, will often strike root into the ground and form a circle of young trees round the parent one.

84. **THE HEMLOCK SPRUCE FIR** (*A. Canadensis*).—This is a very handsome ornamental tree, from Canada, of a pendulous habit, for which it is esteemed, but it does not answer to grow as a timber tree, and is not very extensively cultivated.

85. **THE WHITE AMERICAN SPRUCE FIR** (*A. alba*).—This variety was also introduced into Britain at the close of the seventeenth century, being a native of the same districts as the black spruce fir, in comparison with which it is a far less useful tree in every respect, being of inferior growth, and not nearly so handsome in appearance.

86. **MISCELLANEOUS SPRUCE TREES.**—There are several more very interesting varieties, as *A. Brunoniana*, which has come to us from the Himalayas, which bears a strong family likeness to the hemlock spruce, and forms a very ornamental tree, with pendant branches and silvery foliage; but its growth is too feeble to be useful as a forest tree. Another is the Khutrow, or Marinda (*A. Smithiana*), known also as the Himalayan spruce fir, which was imported into this country in 1818. The tree is a very beautiful one when in perfect health, but it generally becomes diseased before it attains to the dimensions of a timber-tree.

The varieties we have mentioned of the cone-bearing trees embrace the leading species which are employed either for ornamental planting or profit. When it is considered how easily trees can be established in barren and unproductive situations, and waste pieces of land, that are often eyesores, can be made to become profitable, clothed with objects of beauty, the importance of the subject will be readily recognized, as well as the necessity for acting upon the suggestions proffered.

CHAPTER IV.

GROWING OSIERS.

Osiers—Laying down an Osier-bed—Action of Light upon Osiers—Mending Osier-beds—Time for Cutting Osiers—The Trade Preparation of Osiers.

There are numerous patches of land by the sides of rivers, especially those that are flooded by almost every tide, that are quite useless for growing any ordinary crops upon, which may be rendered very profitable by being converted into osier-beds.

But in the formation of them it is necessary to select the best kind of willow, or osier, adapted to each situation. Osiers grow to the greatest perfection on strong, rich, and loamy soils, not succeeding so well on strong clayey ones, because these in summer time become dry and hard, and full of cracks, through which the moisture evaporates.

Osier-beds in the best situations have been known to stand for seventy years, but in the lighter soils, with only an imperfect supply of moisture, they are not of more than from fifteen to twenty years duration, when they require to be laid down afresh.

On the banks of the Severn, osiers grow to great perfection, the height of the tides for which that river is famous exercising a beneficial influence upon them. Some of the best osiers which supply the London market are grown on the banks of the Thames and Kennet, in Berkshire and Oxfordshire, none exceeding those in size which are raised on the Thames between Chelsea and Richmond, the soil on the banks of this portion of the river being naturally rich, on account of the overflow leaving upon them a top-dressing of rich mud.

87. **LAYING DOWN AN OSIER-BED.**—The ground should be first trenched fifteen or sixteen inches deep, and the sets for planting cut into pieces about fifteen inches long, which are planted at various distances from each other, according to the quality of the land.

In light soils where there is a limited supply of water, when the shoots will be fewer and shorter, it is the common practice to plant them in rows a foot and a half from each other, the sets standing fifteen or sixteen inches apart in the rows, and inserted up to half their length in the ground. If planted at a greater distance, instead of drawing one another up straight, which is the great object in osier growing, they would turn out crooked, thick and clubby at the stools, full of branching twigs above.

But in the richer and stronger soils it is usual to plant them in rows two feet apart, and sixteen or eighteen inches from one another in the rows, as in favourable situations they will attain a height of eight, ten, twelve, or even thirteen feet. If planted as thickly on the rich soils as in the poor, there would not be sufficient space for the number of shoots the plants would throw out, the result of which would be that the leading shoots would be drawn up very tall, and prevent the light acting upon the others, so that the wood would not become ripened, but be soft and pithy, and unfit for the purpose of basket-making.

88. **ACTION OF LIGHT UPON OSIERS.**—The action of light has a very marked effect upon the shoots of osiers in different seasons. In some they will be of a yellowish brown, which is its proper or natural colour, in others the osier will be of a dull green. In clear seasons willows are of a bright cherry red, but in cloudy ones they are of a dull mahogany colour.

A good deal of confusion prevails as to the names of the various species of osiers, the best variety of the *Salix viminalis* bearing the several ones of "The Brindled Osier," "Blotched Osier," "Snake Osier," and "Speckled Osier," all being identical and the same. The shoots of the osier are generally called "rods" by the basket makers. The common osier, being coarse, soft, and brittle, and not liked by them, is now almost thrown out of cultivation.

89. **THE GREEN-LEAVED OSIER, OR ORNARD** (*Salix rubra*). —This is an excellent and tough variety; with the bark on, it is considered the best for making carboy baskets.

90. **THE SPANIARD, OR SPANIARD ROD** (*Salix triandra*).— There are several varieties of this species, some possessing excellent

qualities; others, again, being nearly worthless. The *Black-budded Spaniard* is considered the best kind for bottoming and finishing the rims and handles of farmers' baskets. The *Grey Spaniard* is considered fit for coarse brown baskets, as well as the *Brown Spaniard*, but the *Horse Spaniard* is of very inferior quality.

91. **THE BLUNT-LEAVED ORNARD** (*Salix Lambertiana*), **ROSE ORNARD** (*Salix helix*), **BASTARD FRENCH** (*Salix lanceolata*), take rank only with the inferior kinds, being mostly used for coarse hampers and fishing baskets, and objectionable on account of the numerous snapped ends which project from the articles made, in consequence of their brittleness in working.

92. **THE BITTER ORNARD** (*Salix purpurea*) grows slender and tough, and is well adapted for very wet ground, like all the other ornards, all of which grow in water.

The rods called *willows* by the basket-makers near London are of a reddish hue, and comprise several varieties. First, the willow commonly known by that designation, and a variety termed the *Skit willow*. The *Yellow*, or *Dutch willow*, which, although occasionally used for baskets, is seldom grown for that purpose, being mostly consumed as *withes*, or *withies*, for tying up bundles of various productions. These are soaked in water when they lose their natural sap after being cut. This is the chief reason why the *Dutch willow* is so little esteemed, not only because it grows rough and twiggy, but on account of its softness, which will not allow it to bear soaking, as the others do.

93. **THE BROWN ROD, BROWNARD, OR SILVER OSIER** (*Salix Hoffmanniana*).—This variety is silvery on the underside of the leaf, being short but firm, and useful for certain kinds of basket-making.

94. **GELSTER** is similar to the Spaniard in quality, but the butt end is thicker, and it grows in a more tapering form.

95. **THE NEW KIND** (*Salix Forbyana*) also resembles the Spaniard, being very strong, but is more pliable and therefore more easily worked.

96. **THE FRENCH, FRENCH ROD, OR REAL FRENCH**, so termed from its having been imported from France, where it is much used, is a good variety for small, fine work extensively used in France for twigs for binding wooden hoops on coopers' wine casks, &c., being also used largely in the manufacture of small baskets.

Besides those of the variety of the *Salix viminalis* first named, there are the *Yellow-barked osier*, the *Velvet-topped*, and *Apple-tree osier*, as well as the *Long-skin*, which is of smaller growth, but its wood is heavier, firmer, and tougher.

Rods (osiers, &c.) are said to grow to the greatest perfection on strong, rich, and loamy soils. They have been also known to succeed very well in marshy land, consisting of a mixture of peat, there being some sorts, such as the French, Goldstone, and a variety of the Spaniard (which in Berkshire passes under the soubriquet of *Black Jack*), which will arrive at tolerable perfection in light soil in which there is a considerable portion of sand. But in such situations their profitable cultivation is somewhat doubtful, as they require a stronger staple, and also a compact sub-soil, in order to retain the moisture which is so essential to them during their growth. For the larger sort of osiers the sets are cut from the lower part of the shoots, or rods, generally about the thickness of the little finger; for although the sets from the small end strike very readily, they always throw out comparatively small shoots.

97. **MENDING OSIER-BEDS.**—When mild winters are succeeded by cold frosty weather in March and April, it often proves very destructive to osier plants, and many of them have to be replanted, it not being an uncommon circumstance to see stools which have made shoots of the thickness of a man's thumb die off in the following spring without making any effort to throw out any more. The method followed in mending plantations is to select the longest and smoothest rods of the sort required, and after their butt-ends have been cut in a slanting direction they are inserted into the ground beside the dead stool to the depth of eight or nine inches, but are not shortened, as in the case of making a new plantation. If this were done they would be smothered by the shoots of the older stools which surround them; but being left tall they enjoy a full share of the light for a considerable portion of the summer before the others reach so high as to shade them. After two years they are cut back to the height of the old stools. A few of the stools will die every year, and in some seasons when the winters are very severe they will do so to a great extent.

98. **TIME FOR CUTTING OSIERS.**—Osiers may be cut any time between the falling of the leaf and the rising of the sap in spring. They are sometimes cut both before and after this period, but it is not advisable to do so, as it tends to weaken the following crops, more especially when cut late in the spring.

99. **THE TRADE PREPARATION OF OSIERS.**—Those who make a business of osier-growing, after cutting, sort them into the various sorts and sizes for basket-making, separating the long and thick ones from the short and small, the rough from the smooth, &c. Those intended for brown baskets are carefully dried and stacked. If laid up too closely together when green they are liable to heat, and consequently when this takes place become useless for basket-making, as the parts which have got heated decay. If the stack is allowed to get wet after they have been dried they also become injured in a similar manner.

Osiers which are intended for making white baskets require to have their bark removed. After being sorted, they are placed upright in wide and shallow trenches, called pits, in which about four inches of water is contained. Into this water the butt-ends are placed. In country districts a shallow rivulet with a gravelly bottom is often chosen for this purpose, and they are kept in an upright position by posts and rails. The sap rises in the spring, and they will bud and blossom as if planted in the ground. Towards the first or second week in May they will be in full leaf, throwing out their roots freely. The sap is then sufficiently raised to admit of the removal of the bark, which is done by drawing it through an instrument called a *Break*, which causes the bark to burst and separate from the rod.

Sometimes in cold and unseasonable weather there is a difficulty in performing this operation properly, the cold checking the flow of the sap. Another process to bring about the same result is then resorted to which is called *couching*. The rods are laid down in a sheltered spot, well watered, and a large quantity of straw, farm-yard refuse, or anything that will cover them very closely, is then placed over them so as to exclude the air. In about a fortnight they will present much the same appearance as that presented by barley in malting, when the bark will separate freely from the rod. After this they must be placed up against rails which are erected for the purpose, and carefully dried ; and afterwards stacked away under some cover where they will not get wet. If damp when stored away, or water reaches them afterwards, they will receive considerable injury.

OAKS.

CHAPTER V.

HEDGES.

The Hawthorn—Weeding young Hedges—Management of young Fences—Hedging and Ditching—Crab-tree Hedge—The Blackthorn—Beech Hedges—Hornbeam—Maple—Hedges for Wet or Boggy Lands—The Holly—Box—Privet—Arbor Vitæ.

Hedges are formed out of a large variety of trees and shrubs, some of which are better fitted than others for different soils and situations, and with specific objects in view. The old-fashioned, lofty, wide-spreading hedge, sometimes overrunning a fourth of the field in which it was situated, however pleasing an object it may have been as a rural adornment, is now no longer tolerated in modern husbandry, and the neatly trimmed fence, which can be easily kept in order, and which presents no obstacle to the free action of the sun and air, has now to be substituted.

Hedge-fences are made from the following: Hawthorn, crab, poplar, willow, yew, box, arbor vitæ, blackthorn, holly, privet, beech, hornbeam, maple, barberry, furze, broom, alder, sweet-briar, &c. The list is a tolerably long one, and, there being so many kinds to choose from, plants may be found suitable for every kind of soil and situation: to make fences to keep out cattle—for ornamental or garden divisions—some adapted for wet or boggy soils, others for those of a dry and sandy nature, and others, again, adapted for general purposes, some being evergreen and some deciduous.

100. **THE HAWTHORN.**—The hawthorn is considered, for general purposes, the most suitable for hedges and fences of all trees and shrubs; from its quick growth, and stubborn, rigid character, adapting itself to most soils. It is a deciduous tree, a native of England, ripening its seeds, by which it is propagated. The *haws*, as they

are called, should be gathered in October. They do not vegetate the first year, and as soon as gathered must be laid in a heap to rot, being spread out rather thinly at first to prevent them from heating; afterwards they are put into a heap, and mixed with sand or fine mould, in the proportion of one third of the whole. The heap should be covered over with soil from two to three inches thick, and remain in this condition till the time of sowing, the best season being the months of October and November. Many, however, delay the sowing until spring, considering the seed to be less liable to suffer from the weather in winter, and the depredations of mice, &c. The autumn sowing is, however, considered to produce the finest crop.

The soil most suitable for the hawthorn is a rich light loam, although it will grow in almost any description, provided it be not too wet, a moderately damp soil suiting it better than a very dry one. A very light, gravelly, or sandy soil is not suitable for a seedling crop, as the plants are liable to be burnt up before they are strong enough to resist the heat of the sun. Plants are raised in beds four feet wide, or are sown in drills, the latter method being considered the best, the seed-furrows or drills being about sixteen inches apart, and an inch and a half in depth. The seeds are not separated from the sand with which they have been mixed, but are sown with it. About half a peck of seed to every twenty yards will be enough. The seed should be covered over with a rake, but the surface of the bed not made smooth, it being less apt to cake and make a thin crust from alternate rain and sunshine, and so cause the bed to be impervious to the natural play of the elements.

As soon as the young plants make their appearance the rows require to be hoed between, and when they are large enough they should be hand-weeded. A bushel of seed, properly sown and managed, will produce about 4,000 plants, and often many more. They will vary a good deal in size after one season's growth, but an average of from six to nine inches is considered a fair one.

In November the young *quicks*, as they are called, should be transplanted into nursery lines. The method termed *spade-planting* is perhaps the best one to employ, which is done by opening a trench six or eight inches deep, and placing the plants in it singly, at the rate of from eighteen to twenty-four plants to the yard. The roots of the young plants should be shortened a little, in order to induce bushiness of fibre, before being inserted in the lines.

In establishing hedges several methods are followed in planting. Sometimes it is done on a level surface, on the side of a raised bank, and on the top of a bank.

Some like a ditch, while others consider a ditch unnecessary; but whichever method is followed, the soil of the intended site of the hedge should be trenched two spits deep if it will admit of it, three or four feet wide, and a coat of well-rotted manure lightly forked in, which is best done some time before planting.

The site of the fence should be marked out in a straight line by putting some stakes into the ground about twenty yards asunder; one foot from the side where the ditch is intended to be a line should be stretched, and one side of the ditch cut out with a sharp spade. The width of the intended ditch should be then measured, and the further side cut out. Then the top spit should be taken off in squares about six inches deep, and, if pasture-land, they should be turned upside down on the space left between the inner edge of the ditch and the stakes which mark the line where the quick is intended to stand, which will form a support when the plants are inserted. A furrow should then be made three inches deep in a line with the stakes, just at the inner side of the sod, in which the roots of the hedge plants are to be inserted.

The tops of the plants should be cut off with a sharp knife about three inches above the soil mark, which will show itself on the stems, and the tap roots should be also shortened, but none of the small fibres removed. The plants should then be placed in the trench six inches from one another, and the roots carefully inserted without being squeezed or forced in. The soil which has been trenched and manured should then be drawn to the roots to keep them in their proper places. Another spit should then be dug from the top soil of the intended ditch, which, after being well broken up, should be levelled to the stems of the plants, and trod firmly down. The remainder of the soil that is taken out of the ditch can either be levelled in behind the hedge on the field side, or carted away.

Where the land is sufficiently dry, and there are materials easily obtainable for temporary fences, the ditch may be dispensed with. Posts and rails are sometimes used as a protection while the young fence is growing, but these are, of course, expensive.

In wet soils the hedge is sometimes put above the level of the surface, by raising the ground with the soil excavated from the ditch. The plants thus lie dry, and air has access to them, and the rain will sink gradually to their roots.

Another method is, to plant the hedge on the top of a bank, but the plants in this case are somewhat exposed to the weather. The frosts of winter pulverise the soil, which crumbles away from the roots, leaving them too much exposed to the action of the sun's rays and the wind, so that in weak places in the bank some of the plants die, and gaps in the hedge ensue.

101. **WEEDING YOUNG HEDGES.**—When the quicks have been planted and weeds begin to make their appearance, the ground should be well hoed over on both sides of the young hedge, so as to destroy the weeds and loosen the soil at the same time, and also filling up any cracks or inequalities. This should be done not later than the second week in April, when the weeds being young will be easily destroyed, and less risk incurred of injuring the young quicks. The hoeing must be repeated in the summer, and also in the autumn, it being a bad plan to allow the weeds to smother the quick before hoeing is commenced, for they rob the hedge of a great share of the nourishment it would otherwise receive; and with increased age the stems get harder, and men sometimes chop away at them with a spade, by which the roots of the young hedge are often injured and gaps made to begin with, the hoe being a lighter and better implement to make use of.

102. **MANAGEMENT OF YOUNG FENCES.**—A very diversified practice exists with respect to the management of young fences, some cutting and trimming them at the end of the first year, a plan which others denounce as injurious, and who will not allow their own to be touched till the third, fourth, or fifth year, as the case may be. Circumstances must, however, be taken into account, and the nature of the wood which forms the hedge be consulted. In the case of the thorn, it is naturally a low-growing tree, which if left to itself would assume a broad head and a narrow bottom, so that the centre shoots need to be kept down to strengthen the lower ones; and as this cannot be effected when the tree is old it must be done when young. The soil, too, is so variable along a line of fence, that some portions grow stronger than others, and it is thought good practice to take off the tops of luxuriant growers to the height of the weakened ones, after the first year, to prevent their overtopping them during the second year of their growth.

When the plants do not rise more than a foot high during the first season, it is not desirable to cut at all, but when they exceed a foot, perhaps it is best to switch off the tops to the height of a foot or a foot and a half, according to their strength. It will be found that moderate pruning will do no harm to the plants whatever at that height; it is only when unmerciful pruning is resorted to that damage ensues.

If, on the other hand, a hedge is left too long unpruned, it is apt to get bare at the bottom. Good managers of hedges recommend topping again the second year according to its strength, one foot, or a foot and a half above last year's cutting, at the same time cutting off the tops of any side shoots which may extend more than fifteen or eighteen inches from the stems of the plants, which not only thickens the hedge, but prevents accidents from the weight of snow falling upon them, and other causes, which are apt to injure the fence. The third year the same process will require to be repeated, the hedger striking his switching-bill upwards, directing his stroke from the bottom gradually to the centre. The argument for the adoption of this line of practice is, that if by cutting early a little of the strength of the stem is lost, a more than sufficient compensation is gained by the stout, stubborn face the hedge acquires.

After the third year an annual cutting will be required to keep the hedge in good order. October or March are the best months for doing this, though a great many farmers make it a rule to cut their hedges between haytime and harvest, the wood being softer and more easily cut than when it is destitute of leaves; but by cutting off the leaves and branches before the descent of the sap some of the means by which the plant supports itself in a healthy state are taken away, by preventing the return of the sap to the root, which would help to maintain it the ensuing year.

At ten, twelve, or fifteen years, the natural habit of the hawthorn will assert itself, and show its disposition to assume the form of a tree, according to the nature of the soil in which it is planted, when it will be required to be cut down wholly or in part.

103. **HEDGING AND DITCHING.**—The operation of cutting the hedge, and cleaning out the ditch, is called "hedging and ditching," the cutting being performed in different ways, according to the condition and requirements of the hedge. They are sometimes cut down entirely to the surface, in order to renew them; are laid and plashed with the same intention, but also to retain and secure a fence more readily; and are cropped after being cut down, or laid and plashed to restrain their growth and keep them within a limited space. They are also occasionally *breasted*, a term which is applied when they are cut off about three and a half to four feet high. The cutting down to the surface is adopted after a hedge has been laid and plashed, or cropped so long that symptoms of decay begin to exhibit themselves, it being an effectual method of restoring a hedge where there are sufficient roots left to make young shoots enough to form a fence free from gaps.

104. **CRAB-TREE HEDGE.**—The crab is generally reckoned next to the hawthorn in point of usefulness as a hedge-plant, but it has not the rigid character which distinguishes the former, and is more subject to the attacks of blight and vermin, while, from its unaccommodating disposition, it is much more difficult to repair it.

The fruit, or crabs, ripen in October, when they need to be laid in a heap to rot, so as to separate the seed from the pulp, and to remain in that state during the winter, being turned over two or three times in the meanwhile, in order to assist the operation. The seed should be sown in March, it being previously rubbed with a little sand between the hands to free them from the rotten mass, so that they may be evenly sown, which is done in the same way as the thorn.

The plants should stand in rows fifteen inches apart in nursery lines, and two or three inches from each other. The stoutest can be planted out after standing one year, but the weaker ones will have to remain for two or three years. They must be planted in the fence entire, and not be cut down until they have stood for a year in the position they are to occupy.

A similar course of management is recommended to that of the thorn. The crab will be found a good plant for filling up gaps in old hedges: they throw out numerous shoots, which frequently reach four or five feet the first year, being bushy and strong in proportion.

105. **THE BLACKTHORN** (*Prunus spinosa*).—The sprays of the blackthorn are neither so numerous nor so sharp as those of the hawthorn, and do not in consequence form so good a hedge, though from the great number of remains of hedges which may be seen, it was evidently a favourite hedge-plant with our forefathers.

It is, however, of free growth and very hardy, and will do well in a damp soil and more exposed situation than the hawthorn, and, like the crab, is most useful in filling up gaps in hedges. Unless, however, the plants are raised from seed they are very liable to throw out suckers.

The sloes, or fruit, should be gathered in October, and be placed in a heap to rot until spring, and may be sown any time not later than March, the same method of cultivation as in the case of the hawthorn being followed. The young seedlings will require to be placed in nursery lines at one year old, and will generally be strong enough to plant out after having stood one year in lines. They must never, however, be allowed to remain more than a year in the seed-bed, having a tap root, which is likely to be injured. A second crop will occasionally appear equal to the first.

106. **BEECH HEDGES.**—The beech (*Fagus sylvatica*) makes a capital hedge, retaining its leaves during winter in a withered state. In exposed situations round farmyards a beech fence is often found very useful. The directions for raising the plants we have

given under the head of the beech tree, so that we shall not have occasion to recapitulate them here; but in marking out the position for the fence it will be necessary to dig over the ground from two to three feet wide, and sufficiently deep to admit the roots without injury. The plants should be inserted one foot apart, and placed so as to cross one another in the same way as a lattice fence, and any side shoots which appear to need it should be removed. As the fence grows, the leading shoots which appear to be getting stronger than the adjoining plants should be cut off, to induce an equal growth. The best season for trimming or cutting beech hedges is in the summer, about July.

107. **THE HORNBEAM** (*Carpinus betulus*).—We have also previously described the specialties of the hornbeam, which on the whole is considered to be inferior to the beech as a hedge-plant, refusing to grow on some soils where the latter would flourish. On chalky soils it never answers, though on loams and clay it is often found to do well enough.

108. **MAPLE** (*Aceraceæ campestre*).—The maple makes but an inferior hedge-plant, not affording much shelter, and is also deficient in strength, but maple hedges are sometimes to be met with, so they demand a cursory notice, which will bring to an end the list of deciduous trees which are fit for hedge-plants, suitable for somewhat high and dry grounds.

109. **HEDGES FOR WET OR BOGGY LANDS.** — Hedges for wet or boggy lands may be made from the willow, birch, alder, and elder. The alder is propagated from seed, and the three others from cuttings. The shoots are divided into lengths of about a foot, which are stuck into the ground along the line of the intended fence. They will mostly grow readily enough, and give but little trouble in their management.

110. **THE HOLLY** (*Ilex aquifolium*).—The holly makes a most beautiful and durable hedge, and no plant will better repay any trouble which may be taken with it. The time required for bringing a holly hedge to maturity will vary somewhat according to circumstances, but on an average it will be eight to ten years before it gets four or five feet high.

The holly will grow almost anywhere except in a wet soil, and will allow itself to be over-shadowed by other trees, and, in a picturesque point of view, is superior to all other hedge plants, being clothed with shining evergreen foliage throughout the year.

The seeds are ripe in December, when they should be gathered and laid in a heap to rot, until the second succeeding March or April (fifteen or sixteen months), when they should be sown in light mould in beds, and covered with about a quarter of an inch of the lightest soil which is procurable. The plants make but very slow progress the first year, and require to be sheltered from the sun.

After standing in the bed for five years they need to be planted in nursery lines one foot apart, the plants standing two or three inches from one another in rows. After having stood in the nursery lines two, or at most four years, they must be again transplanted a foot and a half from each other in the rows, and eight inches from plant to plant, where they must remain two years more. As it is of the greatest importance to give them fibrous roots, it is well to plant them out once more, increasing the distance, before they are finally put out to form the hedge.

The ground where the future hedge is to stand should be well trenched and manured, and the plants put into the ground during the months of May, August, or September. The best time for cutting or trimming the holly (as well as most other evergreen plants) is after frost disappears in the spring, or during the summer. If cut in July, the aftergrowth hides the marks which have been made by the shears. Cutting should never be practised at the end of autumn or beginning of winter, as the stems of the plants become exposed to the frost, by which they suffer injury. Weeds will hardly grow beneath it; cattle will not eat it; and when closely cut, birds can scarcely force their way through. The great drawback is the long time it takes to reach maturity, though when the fence is but small it forms a very effectual barrier against aggressors.

111. **THE FURZE** (*Ulex Europæus*).—This, though a somewhat inferior hedge-plant, is made very useful in certain localities, especially in sandy or elevated districts where other plants will not thrive. Its appearance is very ornamental, being covered with handsome yellow blossoms for a great portion of the year. The best method of cultivation is to throw up a bank two and a half or three feet high, flattened at the top, on which the seeds should be sown in a drill or furrow, in the month of March or beginning of April. The first year the plants will grow from nine inches to a foot high. They should not be interfered with the first year, but should be topped over with the shears in the second, in either April or May, and the operation repeated every year. They may be cut any time during the summer months, but not in the winter, when they are apt to suffer from frost. By constant summer pruning the furze will be prevented from getting bare and appearing dead at the bottom.

112. **BOX** (*Buxus sempervirens*).—The box is thoroughly hardy, and resists the severest cold in winter, but is easily affected by the frosts during the first year of its growth. Plants are seldom propagated by seed, but raised from cuttings, which should be planted in September in a sandy soil, and partially shaded. It forms a very compact evergreen hedge, and admits of being freely pruned at any season, the end of June being the most appropriate time for this

operation to be performed, as it will immediately throw out a few leaves after that time, which will obliterate the marks of the shears. There are several varieties of gold and silver-edged box, which, when freely grown in a shady situation, lose their variegated appearance, and get assimilated to the common tree.

113. **PRIVET** (*Ligustrum*).—The privet plant is deciduous when found growing in a wild state in woods and hedges, but in its cultivated habit becomes evergreen. It varies in the form of its leaves, flowers, and fruit, the same as most plants which have remained for a long time under cultivation.

The berries remain in the bush during the winter, forming handsome purple clusters, which are not generally eaten by birds unless the winters are unusually severe. It is a very hardy plant, and will thrive in almost any soil or situation, standing the smoke of towns well, and under the drip of trees; but in order to produce good flowers it must be situated in an open situation. The Chinese privet, or wax-tree, produces from its berries a kind of vegetable wax somewhat resembling that from the *Myrica cirifera.*

BOX TREE.

114. **THE BARBERRY** (*Berberis vulgaris*). — This plant was formerly met with in great quantities in the hedgerows of England, but has almost universally been banished, from the belief that its presence was injurious to the neighbouring crops; and although this has been often regarded as a vulgar prejudice only, the fact remains that the fructification of the barberry is not complete unless the stamens be irritated by insects. The flowers are peculiarly attractive to insects, and in this way the barberry may become injurious to neighbouring plants.

115. **ARBOR VITÆ** (*Thuja occidentalis*).—A well-known evergreen shrub in this country only, but in Canada, its native locality, it grows to the height of a tree, the wood being considered more durable than that of most others. It makes a handsome hedge, but is merely resorted to on account of its highly ornamental character.

CHAPTER VI.

TIMBER SUITABLE FOR HEDGEROWS.

Establishing Trees in Exposed Situations — Selection of Varieties—Planting Hedgerow Trees—Pruning Hedgerow Trees.

The quantity of timber grown along the sides of roads, in hedges, and in the division of fields in England, is supposed to be much greater in the aggregate than that produced in close woods and forests. The importance of hedgerow timber, it is thought, is generally somewhat underrated in this country therefore.

Although in some situations there are, without doubt, far too many trees, yet in others there is a great deficiency in this respect; a want of the shelter and embellishment which timber can furnish is felt. In some exposed situations in Scotland, where gales are of frequent occurrence in the end of June or beginning of July, a good deal of injury is often sustained by the turnip crop, as they not only disturb and injure the young plants, but actually drift them away, this casualty being most severely felt when rough weather ensues immediately after the young plants have been singled out.

116. **ESTABLISHING TREES IN EXPOSED SITUATIONS.**—Where there are very bleak and weather-beaten tracts of cultivated land, which lie much exposed, the cultivation of timber trees cannot be recommended, unless plantations of some little breadth are formed on all exposed points, in order that single trees may grow freely. It is only under the protection of such beltings that in many districts single lines of trees can be successfully cultivated. Unless the severity of the blast is tempered, hedgerow trees will fail to attain the size which will cause them to be valuable as timber.

117. **SELECTION OF VARIETIES.**—In all windy situations plants should be chosen which are stout in proportion to their height, with lateral branches extending down to the ground. In England, perhaps, the English elm is the most commonly cultivated

as a hedgerow tree. It forms a bushy root when a plant, and when properly managed admits of removal at a size beyond that of most trees. Its figure is erect, and the spread of its branches do not too much overshadow the growing crops. It admits of being frequently lopped, and forms a useful pollard, yielding much timber in a short space of time. The suckers we have previously described, which the tree is apt to produce, forms a slight disadvantage to its being used by the sides of cultivated fields, but a supply of young plants may at all events be obtained through this habit.

The oak, next to the elm, is generally chosen for a hedgerow tree, for although not standing so erect as the English elm, as their roots strike deeper down than those of most other trees, they are less destructive to the crops in their vicinity, being less dependent upon the surface soil for their support; while being late in expanding their leaves, they do not overshadow the crops in their immediate neighbourhood during the early part of the season. The Turkey oak grows the fastest, and retains an upright figure until very old, but is less valuable as a timber tree than most other oaks. All the common varieties of oak are very suitable for hedgerows.

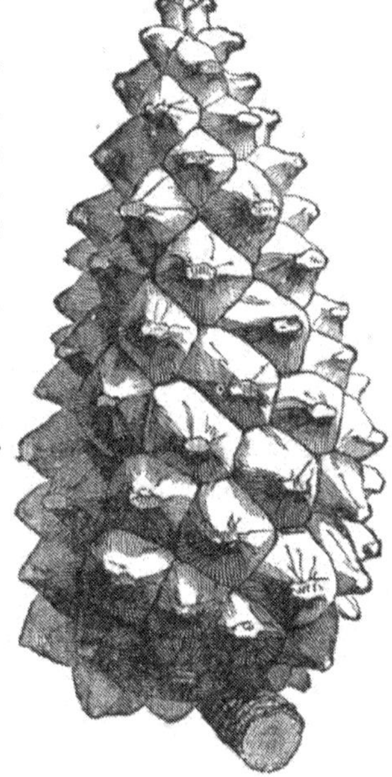

PINE CONE.

The ash may frequently be seen figuring as a hedgerow tree in many districts, but it is ruinous to grain crops in the immediate vicinity of its roots, where sowing and reaping is in vain. But it is appropriate in the absence of tillage along road sides, meadow, and pasture land, &c., while as a timber tree for agricultural purposes it has no superior.

The larch, though seldom found in the hedgerows of highly cultivated districts which are possessed of a superior climate, is nevertheless a very suitable tree, and deserves to be made more frequent use of than falls to its lot in this way, forming an agreeable variety, and breaking the monotonous appearance of some districts. Being of rapid growth, it is profitable and valuable as timber, and is also less subject to disease when standing in isolated positions. Its leaves enrich the soil when shed, commonly being deposited on the surface around its roots, no tree being less injurious to grain crops. There is a drawback, however, to its being placed in rough situations, as it is apt to be bent by the prevailing winds and become unsightly.

For those places which are too rough and exposed for most trees, the sycamore service tree, beech, Scotch elm, mountain ash, and hoary poplar are the most likely to succeed. The sycamore, service tree, and mountain ash are best adapted for cold and windy situations, being very unyielding in disposition, even at elevations of great exposure growing erect and maintaining well balanced heads.

Of evergreen trees, the different varieties of holly and oak are the best adapted for hedgerows. The tallest growing are Turner's evergreen oak, and the Fulham oak, a sub-evergreen.

When a depth of embowering shade and seclusion is required, the lime tree with its umbrageous head, yielding sweet-smelling blossoms, has no superior. The horse-chestnut, too, is also a very appropriate tree in such situations, as well as the Spanish chestnut, sycamore, Scotch elm, beech, and planes, which, all being of a spreading habit, recommend themselves for this adaptation.

118. **FLOWERING HEDGEROW TREES.**—Among the flowering trees adapted for ornament are the varieties of thorn, laburnum, lilac, and scarlet horse-chestnut, all of which make a beautiful appearance. Lines of the scarlet hawthorn may be rapidly produced by choosing strong stems of the common hawthorn from a vigorous growing hedge, which may be readily trained to a considerable height, when they may be grafted with the varieties and species of the tree. Those having the most handsome and attractive flowers are the scarlet and double red, and for habit of growth, blossom, and ornamental fruit the kinds most esteemed are *Cratægus macracantha*, *C. prunifolia*, *C. glandulosa*, *C. punctata*, *C. coccinea*, and *C. aronia.*

119. **PLANTING HEDGEROW TREES.**—In planting hedgerow timber, for the first few years after the trees have been inserted the surface of the ground needs to be kept well loosened and clear of herbage—points which are very often neglected—to the extent of the space which would comprehend the spreading roots of the tree. In planting them their roots should not be sunk under the surface beyond their natural depth, the upper fibres of the root requiring to be so situated as to feel the influence of every shower.

120. **PRUNING HEDGEROW TREES.**—When trees are grown in plantations or the forest, their proximity to one another generally does away with the necessity for much pruning, as a tendency to grow with bare trunks is thus encouraged; but the case is different when they are situated singly, and the mode of pruning, under any circumstances of great importance, is never more so than when placed in hedgerows; and no part of their management demands more skilful attention. Pruning should be done early, so that there is no necessity for the removal of large branches.

It has been commonly remarked that the method of pruning trees for useful purposes appears generally to be imperfectly understood; or at all events, if understood, to be very seldom carried out; the common method being to strip the trunk of all lateral branches to a considerable height, and allow the higher ones to take what course they please. This tends to cause the tree to make a large head, widely spread and ramified, and should this figure of growth be wanted there is no better way of accomplishing it, as it has the effect of producing numerous branches almost equal in magnitude to the leader, which retards the height and adds to the breadth of the tree. But where a great bulk of timber is aimed at, the mode of treatment should be very different. It then becomes necessary to direct attention chiefly to the top or leading shoot and the branches in its vicinity, with the view of continuing the length of the trunk, and so concentrating the strength of the tree as to prevent it from dividing into forks or clefts.

This is best done by preserving one leading shoot, and by shortening the competing ones, or those which bear a considerable proportion to the leader, to about half their length; and the same method is recommended to be followed in dealing with all luxuriant side-branches throughout the tree, the progress of such branches being impeded in a greater or lesser degree in proportion to the distance from the extremities at which they are cut. By this course of procedure the principal flow of sap will be directed in the proper channel, which will greatly increase the height of the trunk; and the remaining portions of the side-branches may be removed close from the trunk, in after years, when they will occasion no blemish in the timber, by reason of their being still of small diameter.

September is generally the best month for pruning, as then the wounds are immediately healed by the descending sap. The timber of detached trees is generally hard and good, and if cleanly grown, by being early and judiciously pruned, it invariably sells at as high a price as the clean timber which has been grown in a forest. The value, on the other hand, is frequently depreciated forty per cent. if it is coarse, with large knots, or has been mutilated by the removal of large branches. In some districts the value of hedgerow timber is often reduced very greatly by the mischievous practice of nailing paling to trees, in order to save the trouble of inserting stakes. It commonly happens that the nails become imbedded in the timber, which is only discovered when the carpenter's tools come into contact with them in cutting it up.

CHAPTER VII.

PLANTATIONS.

North American Trees—Modern Plantations—Draining—Ridging—The Formation of Plantations—Methods of Planting—Notch Planting—Pit Planting—Prepared Ground for Planting—Hardwood Plantations—Thinning.

Almost every year adds to the number of new trees which are imported into England, but the first half of the present century was very much enriched by the addition of new varieties, particularly in the *coniferæ*.

North American Trees.—For these we are mainly indebted to the exertions of Douglas, who went to North-west America as a botanical collector, and who introduced to us from the banks of the Columbia the *Abies* (spruce fir) *Douglassi*, *A. amabilis*, *A. grandis*, *A. nobilis*, *Pinus Lambertiana*, and other kinds, which, from the immense size they attain in their native *habitat*, will doubtless prove of great value to the collection of our timber trees, as well as those from the Himalaya mountains, as *Cedrus deodora*, *Pinus excelsa*, &c., &c., which in course of time will doubtless become more common for the formation of plantations than they have hitherto been; a century, at all events, being wanted to elapse before the positive results in connection with different trees can be safely determined upon.

The number of species of foreign plants introduced into Britain during the eighteenth century amounted to nearly five hundred, but the fourth of these were shrubs, more than half of them being natives of North America. The timber trees consisted chiefly of oaks, pines, poplars, maples, and thorns; and many large plantations were formed in different parts of the country, though it was during the sixteenth century that plantations began to be extensively formed for timber and embellishment.

121. **MODERN PLANTATIONS.**—During the present century the Highland and Agricultural Society of Scotland has been the means of spreading plantations through the country, by offering premiums for the production of new timber, and for extensive plantations throughout Scotland. It is reported by that institution that the Earl of Seafield planted upwards of thirty millions of young trees, in a space exceeding eight thousand acres; and extensive planting has been carried on by various landed proprietors since that report.

122. **DRAINING.**—It is seldom that any space of ground of any extent can be found adapted for planting which does not require some part of it, at all events, to be drained. Open ditches are considered best for this purpose, but as it sometimes happens that an open ditch cannot always be formed, owing to the depth required in some parts to form an exit for the water, and the great width required at the surface to form a sufficient slope on the sides, the best method is to build an eye of stone or to introduce a tile pipe to carry it off, young plants recently formed being more apt to suffer from want of drainage than plantations which are more advanced. Trees, particularly the pine tribe, when they have become sufficiently advanced to form a cover to the ground, have a tendency to dry it, by intercepting the showers and ordinary humidity of the atmosphere, so that the drainage which may have been necessary at the first establishment of the plantation may afterwards be dispensed with.

123. **RIDGING.**—When land cannot very well be properly drained, the mode of ridging is sometimes resorted to, particularly in soils surcharged with water; which is done by excavating every alternate space five or six feet in breadth, the part which forms the ridge being thus raised in the same proportion as the depth of the excavation. This operation should be performed in summer and the plants be set out in spring.

124. **THE FORMATION OF PLANTATIONS.**—The methods followed in the formation of plantations are exceedingly diversified, which naturally arises from the difference of the soil and the nature of the herbage which overspreads it. On the soil and exposure must depend the kind of plants that are to be employed, and the quality of the herbage must determine the size and description of the plants, which require to be adapted to the soil most congenial to their growth.

125. **METHODS OF PLANTING.**—There are three methods of planting practised throughout the country: first, the *notch*, or *slit*

method of planting; secondly, *pit planting;* and lastly, in trenched or prepared ground.

126. **NOTCH PLANTING.**—This method is extensively practised in Scotland, and although it is often considered a very coarse operation by English planters, who have not the same conditions of soil and herbage to deal with, yet in dry, gravelly, or sandy moorland, with a cover of open heath not exceeding four or five inches in height, it is not only the most speedy method of planting, but also the most effective and economical.

It is not practised with plants of great size, but is adapted for Scotch pines and spruce two-year-old seedlings, or for the same one-year-old transplanted, and for other plants not exceeding them in size. The best implement for this purpose is the small planting spade or hand-iron, the blade of which is about seven inches long, its weight about two and a half pounds.

The person using it has a small bag, in which he holds the plants, tied round his waist. The spade is struck into the ground in a slanting direction with one hand, which penetrates more easily than when held perpendicularly, the plant being inserted with the other hand, on the further side of the iron, and by twisting the turf a little to one side with the spade a sufficient opening is made for the roots. When the plant is inserted the ground should receive a stamp with the foot to make it firm. This is better than making a larger opening, as moor or peat ground is naturally apt to contract during the heat of summer, and by making a larger opening it exposes the roots at a time when they are the most apt to suffer. The herbage with which the plants are associated in this case is that of heath, which is more favourable to young trees than if they were planted upon a bare surface, the cover affording protection while its stems do not retain moisture to rot the plant.

When there is a short swarded surface, or other matted, close herbage, seedling pines or firs are not appropriate, but transplanted plants should be used, to which we have made partial reference before, and if inserted by the notch system, it is necessary that a turf be removed from the surface of each spot where the plant is to stand, the turf so removed being about two inches thick, and if the soil is stiff underneath, it should be loosened by a stroke or two of the pick, and after the plant has been *notched* into the ground the turf should be divided, and placed round its stem, with the underside uppermost.

Another method for preparing a land of this description is, to dig over a spadeful of the ground where the plant is to stand, placing the surface in the bottom. In adopting this mode the digging should be done in summer or autumn, and the plants inserted in early spring.

In rough ground where the heath is rank, the hand-iron (the use of which is scarcely known in England) is unsuitable, and the common spade will be found best adapted for planting: in making what is called a "cross-cut," the surface soil is raised, and the plant inserted in the corner, and the turf pressed down with the foot. A spade which has been well worn and is sharp is necessary to perform this operation, a new one being unsuitable; while the plants must be large in proportion to the herbage they have to contend with. If there is any danger of its choking the plant, it should be cut away where the young tree is to be placed, and if the surface is rather close and grassy, a spadeful of the soil should be turned over before inserting the plant.

127. **PIT PLANTING.**—Pits are commonly made eighteen inches wide and fifteen deep, and are usually made for the reception of the two-year-old transplanted hardwood trees, where the soil is deeper, richer, and better sheltered than that usually planted with the species of pines. Pits should be made a few months before the plants are inserted, and in forming them, after the bottom is made quite soft, the surface sward should be filled in, first chopped, and covered up to the depth of five or six inches with the soil; which will be considerably decomposed by the time the plants are placed in them.

It is usual to plant ground dry and moderately sheltered at the beginning of winter, but when the soil is of an opposite description, early in spring during open weather is considered better. In hard soil, the bottom of the pit should be loosened with the pick, and the pit must be made large in proportion to the plants when bigger ones than two-year-old are employed. The larger the pits the better the roots of the trees can be spread, and enjoy a greater amount of loose soil, which is favourable to their early growth.

When the roots are evenly spread in the pit, the earth, which should have been previously well pulverised, is evenly and gently spread over them, and afterwards pressed down by the foot all round the plant, which should stand perpendicularly in the soil, an inch deeper in the ground than it stood in the nursery, which can be readily seen by the ground mark left on the stem.

In finishing the filling up of the pit, it is of great use, particularly in dry soils, to leave a regular concavity around the plant, for the purpose of retaining moisture, which is valuable in establishing newly-planted trees. On the slopes of hill-sides, where the moisture will run off, this is especially necessary, and the outer, or under edge of the pit should be formed sufficiently high to intercept the rain.

128. **PREPARED GROUND FOR PLANTING.** — The most thorough method of insuring success in planting, is to have the ground well trenched. Trenching land is, indeed, an expensive

operation; but a capital crop of roots, such as potatoes or carrots, may often be got off it during the first season of the plantation, which will considerably reduce the expense of the operation, and th advantage arising from ground that has been well trenched is, that trees of a larger size will more readily take root and become established than in ground prepared in any other way. But when plants are of the ordinary size, their growth in six years is generally equal to that in ten years in ground prepared in any other way.

In all prepared ground it is necessary to keep it clear of weeds for two or three years after planting, until the trees make sufficient cover to keep down the surface vegetation, and the expense and labour of doing this is always much smaller on trenched ground, so that the cost of trenching is really much less than at first sight may appear to be.

Dry sandy soil is often overspread with a closely matted herbage, which, without being trenched, renders any mode of planting very uncertain, while trenching will cause it to be reliable, the closeness of the surface sward intercepting the fertilising influence of the showers which fall, and the depth of its fibrous roots being a great hindrance to the growth of young trees.

Furze not unfrequently forms a close cover on good land, which is well adapted for the growth of timber. When the furze is cut or rooted out, the ground may be pitted or the land trenched, the larch being the best tree to form a speedy cover, and extirpate the furze.

129. **HARDWOOD PLANTATIONS.**—In all good soils the oak and the ash may be grown profitably, which are the leading kinds resorted to for plantations, the elm and the sycamore not being so generally grown in masses. An acre of ash, elm, or sycamore, at the age of forty years, is generally found to contain from 2,500 to 3,000 cubical feet of timber, and at sixty years about double that extent of measurable timber. This is exclusive of the thinnings, which are generally removed up to this period, and which often form a source of great profit while the plantations are young.

130. **THINNING.**—The more valuable kinds of broad-leaved trees are generally interspersed with *coniferæ*, generally those of the fastest growth, which serve as nurses when they are young, and promote a better order of growth by preventing their getting into a bushy form. It is sometimes found that a Scotch pine, or any other tree inserted for shelter, presses too closely on a more valuable plant, and yet the shelter cannot altogether be dispensed with. In that case, the branches on the side of the pine should be removed which press too closely, and the tree itself at a subsequent thinning.

The distance at which hardwood should stand in a plantation depends very much upon their luxuriance, considerable loss being frequently sustained by producing tall trunks through confinement, without a proportionate diameter; but thinning should commence in plantations formed at a distance of four feet, when they get twelve to fifteen feet high, by removing the worst, which press too closely upon the others, and fully half the number of plants should be removed per acre, by the time the most valuable portion is twenty feet high.

When they attain the he ght of thirty feet they should stand on an average fully seven feet asunder, or about eight hundred to the acre. At the height of forty feet, when they will be about forty years old, the trunks will have risen to a considerable height, and at this stage of their development it becomes necessary to allow a considerable space for the development of the leaves of the trees which are to occupy the ground finally, in order that their trunks may possess a girth corresponding to their height. Therefore, generally speaking, they should stand from eleven to twelve feet asunder, or at the rate of from 300 to 350 trees per acre.

Unlike the larch and pine woods, the broad-leaved plantations are generally permanent, as young saplings everywhere abound, ready to take the form of timber trees on the removal of the large trees in their vicinity.

The profits derivable from the timber of hardwood trees are generally very great, but they vary exceedingly, being dependent very much upon local demand, and *very much upon the management.*

THE BAOBAB TREE.

CHAPTER VIII.

PLANTING FOR ORNAMENTATION.

Trees for Exposed Situations—The Mountain Ash, or Roman Tree—The Service Tree—Elder—Scarlet-berried Elder—Laburnum—Trees for Park Scenery—Ornamental Hardy Evergreens—Deciduous Trees of Low Growth.

We shall conclude this portion of our work with a brief description of the trees best fitted for ornamental planting, with a short notice of a few trees of which we have not spoken in the preceding pages.

In forming ornamental plantations it is always desirable to have plants of a good size, capable of producing an immediate effect; and in order to enable good sized trees to take root and flourish, it must be borne in mind, what we have insisted upon all along, namely, that their successes will mainly depend upon the roots of the plants being prepared by repeated transplantation while in the nursery ground; and that the situations to which they are removed are favourable to their growth, as respects soil and shelter.

131. **TREES FOR EXPOSED SITUATIONS.**—In exposed situations the following trees furnish good shelter:—Mountain ash, service-tree, common and scarlet elder, Scotch pine, sycamore, aspen, laburnum, beech, and birch. The whole of these will be found useful in situations where there is a difficulty in establishing trees from the bareness of the ground.

132. **THE MOUNTAIN ASH, OR ROWAN TREE** (*Pyrus aucuparia*).—This well-known beautiful tree belongs to the natural order *Rosaceæ*, and is indigenous to the mountainous districts throughout

Europe. It is deciduous, having smooth branches and smooth leaflets, producing its fragrant white blossoms during the months of May and June, which generally change into red berries which become ripe in October. In some of the rocky recesses of its native districts, the tree may be seen almost bending beneath the weight of these scarlet berries.

Although it never reaches a great size, yet it grows very rapidly during the first eight or ten years of its growth, and is possessed of some excellent attributes. It is extremely hardy, and flourishes in a cool soil at a great elevation, where many other trees would die from the amount of exposure to which they were subjected, and is therefore suitable for acting as a nurse to other trees, and in establishing a shelter around buildings in reclaimed land, in bleak and exposed situations, and for rearing plantations of trees of slower growth. At the same time it is possessed of a highly decorative appearance, the beauty of its foliage and its fruit being hardly surpassed by any other tree. Numerous instances could be furnished where the mountain ash and other hardy trees have established a permanent shelter at an altitude of over a thousand feet.

The tree admits of being planted at a height of four feet in a bare situation, generally taking very readily to the ground, and although a deciduous tree, it soon furnishes a considerable amount of shelter from the closeness and number of its branches. As a hedgerow tree in the worst exposures it has no superior. Rising in an upright form even when young, it forms a shapely head which is unaffected by the wind, and its habit of growth remains more fixed and unchangeable than most other trees, some of which are extremely sensitive to altered climatic influences.

It often rises in a wild state associated with the birch, the alder, and the poplar (*P. tremula*), the beauty of its foliage being scarcely surpassed by any other tree.

The mountain ash is propagated from the berries, which become ripe in autumn, when they need to be collected and mixed up with sand, or earth of a light nature, in a pit, where they should be turned over every second or third month, in order that the berries may become entirely decomposed. They should be sown during the second winter or the second spring after they have been collected, in beds composed of rich friable soil. The seeds should be spread upon the surface of the beds, and placed as near as possible together, so as to allow of the young plants coming up about two inches asunder.

At the age of two years the seedlings should be removed into nursery lines two feet from one another, the plants standing in the rows six inches apart. After having stood in the nursery lines for two years, the plants are commonly from four to five feet in height, when they may either be planted out permanently, or shifted into a greater space, so as to fit them for being placed in situations where an immediate effect is wanted.

The finest trees in this kingdom are about forty feet high, with trunks about two feet in diameter. It is said to live for many centuries, and in open situations is very seldom troubled with any disease. Few trees are so ornamental in appearance, and the berries form the food of our singing birds, as the blackbird and thrush. It forms an excellent coppice, and is useful for many special purposes, the bark being possessed of a valuable tanning principle. Its timber is strong and elastic, being close-grained and susceptible of a high polish, being especially valued by the wheelwright for handles for tools, and in turnery.

The species embraces a large number of cultivated varieties, the whole of which are highly ornamental, especially the weeping mountain ash, which when grafted on the top of the common mountain ash, or the service tree, forms an elegant tree that commands universal admiration. There is also a yellow berried variety which is very interesting. Others again differ from the ordinary kind in producing both larger foliage and fruit, but none of the more uncommon kinds attain to the size of a timber tree. All the different varieties yield seed, but can only be certainly reproduced by the process of grafting. Varieties themselves, in the first place, from the original stock, they are apt to return to the old type from which they have strayed, or to assume a different appearance, so that budding, or grafting, must be resorted to, when any special kind is sought to be reproduced.

Pears are frequently grafted upon the mountain ash in Scotland, where the stocks are plentiful and readily obtainable; but though they bear fruit for a few years, they soon become stunted, the stock seldom swelling in equal growth to the graft, so that the union is not by any means a desirable one.

133. **THE SERVICE TREE** *(Pyrus aria).*—This is a hardy tree of great duration, similar in almost every respect to the mountain ash, which it closely resembles, differing in the form of its leaves, which are entire light green above, and downy underneath, which gives it an interesting appearance when agitated by the wind. It grows with great rapidity for the first six or eight years of its life, frequently attaining the height of twelve or sixteen feet in that time, after which it becomes bushy, and the progress of its upward growth becomes slow.

The mode of propagation and treatment suitable for the uncommon ash is adapted to this tree, the timber of both species being very similar.

134. **ELDER** *(S. nigra).* — The common black-berried elder usually attains a height of twenty feet in Britain, yielding a profusion of creamy white blossoms, which when grown extensively emit a somewhat sickening odour. It is useful, however, as a screen-fence in bleak exposures and maritime situations, and is well adapted as a nurse for other trees. It is readily propagated from young shoots. The slips should be from eight to twelve inches long, and inserted about half their length in the ground, any time from the beginning of November till the first of March.

135. **SCARLET-BERRIED ELDER** *(S. racemosa).*—This is by far the most ornamental plant of the genus, and is a native of the middle and south of Europe, and of the mountains of Siberia, where it forms a low tree from twelve to fifteen feet in height. In Britain it attains a greater altitude, possessing all the vigour of the common species, and is equally hardy. In early situations it blossoms about the first of April.

136. **LABURNUM.**—There are two sorts common throughout Britain—*Cytisus laburnum*, the common or English laburnum, and *C. L. alpinus*, the Alpine or Scotch laburnum. Like many of our low trees it grows vigorously during the first few years of its life, being perfectly hardy. It blossoms in May or June, with a richness and profusion of blossom which causes it to be highly esteemed as an embellishment along the margins of plantations and other situations.

The seeds are produced in pods, which become ripe in the winter, and they should be sown in the spring, in light friable ground, two or three inches apart, and covered nearly an inch deep. One-year-old plants are generally a foot high, when they should be transplanted into nursery lines two feet asunder, and the plants one foot distant in the lines. After standing thus for two years, or at most three, they should be removed either into their permanent positions or into a wider space in nursery lines.

137. **TREES FOR PARK SCENERY.**—In situations which admit of trees of a great size being planted, as within the confines of a park or lawn of considerable size, the following will all be found handsome and appropriate.

The British and scarlet American oaks, Fulham oak, cedar of Lebanon, Indian cedar, plane tree, common and purple beech, lime tree, elms of different kinds, horse chestnut, &c.

138. **ORNAMENTAL HARDY EVERGREENS.**—The most hardy trees amongst evergreens adapted to furnish shelter and seclusion in narrow belts, and in various other situations, are the varieties of holly, yew, juniper, evergreen oak, laurel, arbor vitæ, and cedar.

139. **DECIDUOUS TREES OF LOW GROWTH.**—Of the mos

admired kinds of deciduous trees of low growth adapted for ornamental planting, we have a large assortment of thorns, which are much admired, both in the season for blossom and fruit; a variety of laburnum, acacia, lilac, spindle-tree, elder, almond, hazel, cherry, willow, service tree, apple, maple, &c.

In planting, much can be done to heighten ornamental effect by tastefully grouping various trees which present a distinguishing appearance at certain seasons of the year.

The contrast thus displayed by an association of different kinds has a most pleasing result, particularly after the first touch of frost has tinted the foliage of the various deciduous trees.

PINE TREES ON MOUNTAIN SIDE.

INDEX.

(NOTE.—*The references in this Index are to paragraphs. The black figures refer to pages of Illustrations.*)

J. OGDEN AND CO., PRINTERS, 172, ST. JOHN STREET, E.C.

THE PEOPLE'S STANDARD CYCLOPÆDIAS.

EVERYBODY'S LAWYER (Beeton's Law Book). Entirely New Edition, Revised by a BARRISTER. A Practical Compendium of the General Principles of English Jurisprudence: comprising upwards of 14,600 Statements of the Law. With a full Index, 27,000 References, every numbered paragraph in its particular place, and under its general head. Crown 8vo, 1,680 pp., cloth gilt, 7*s*. 6*d*.

*** *The sound practical information contained in this voluminous work is equal to that in a whole library of ordinary legal books, costing many guineas. Not only for every non-professional man in a difficulty are its contents valuable, but also for the ordinary reader, to whom a knowledge of the law is more important and interesting than is generally supposed.*

BEETON'S DICTIONARY OF GEOGRAPHY: A Universal Gazetteer. Illustrated by Maps—Ancient, Modern, and Biblical, and several Hundred Engravings in separate Plates on toned paper. Containing upwards of 12,000 distinct and complete Articles. Post 8vo, cloth gilt, 7*s*. 6*d*.; half-calf, 10*s*. 6*d*.

BEETON'S DICTIONARY OF BIOGRAPHY: Being the Lives of Eminent Persons of All Times. Containing upwards of 10,000 distinct and complete Articles, profusely Illustrated by Portraits. With the Pronunciation of Every Name. Post 8vo, cloth gilt, 7*s*. 6*d*.; half-calf, 10*s*. 6*d*.

BEETON'S DICTIONARY OF NATURAL HISTORY: A Popular and Scientific Account of Animated Creation. Containing upwards of 2,000 distinct and complete Articles, and more than 400 Engravings. With the Pronunciation of Every Name. Crown 8vo, cloth gilt, 7*s*. 6*d*.; half-calf, 10*s*. 6*d*.

BEETON'S BOOK OF HOME PETS: How to Rear and Manage in Sickness and in Health. With many Coloured Plates, and upwards of 200 Woodcuts from designs principally by HARRISON WEIR. With a Chapter on Ferns. Post 8vo, half-roan, 7*s*. 6*d*.; half-calf, 10*s*. 6*d*.

THE TREASURY OF SCIENCE, Natural and Physical. Comprising Natural Philosophy, Astronomy, Chemistry, Geology, Mineralogy, Botany, Zoology and Physiology. By F. SCHOEDLER, Ph.D. Translated and Edited by HENRY MEDLOCK, Ph.D., &c. With more than 500 Illustrations. Crown 8vo, cloth gilt, 7*s*. 6*d*.; half-calf, 10*s*. 6*d*.

A MILLION OF FACTS of Correct Data and Elementary Information concerning the entire Circle of the Sciences, and on all subjects of Speculation and Practice. By Sir RICHARD PHILLIPS. Carefully Revised and Improved. Crown 8vo, cloth gilt, 7*s*. 6*d*.; half-calf, 10*s*. 6*d*.

THE TEACHER'S PICTORIAL BIBLE AND BIBLE DICTIONARY. With the most approved Marginal References, and Explanatory Oriental and Scriptural Notes, Original Comments, and Selections from the most esteemed Writers. Illustrated with numerous Engravings and Coloured Maps. Crown 8vo, cloth gilt, red edges, 8*s*. 6*d*.; French morocco, 10*s*. 6*d*.; half-calf, 10*s*. 6*d*.; Turkey morocco, 15*s*.

THE SELF-AID CYCLOPÆDIA, for Self-Taught Students. Comprising General Drawing; Architectural, Mechanical, and Engineering Drawing; Ornamental Drawing and Design; Mechanics and Mechanism; the Steam Engine. By ROBERT SCOTT BURN, F.S.A.E., &c. With upwards of 1,000 Engravings. Demy 8vo, half-bound, price 10*s*. 6*d*.

London: WARD, LOCK & CO., Salisbury Square, E.C.

(*Continued on Next Page.*)

FAVOURITE AUTHORS, 2/- (*Continued*).

21. **The Squanders of Castle Squander.** By WM. CARLETON.
22. **Forgotten Lives.** By Mrs. NOTLEY.
23. **The Mountain Marriage;** or, The Bandolero. By Captain MAYNE REID.
24. **Debit and Credit.** By GUSTAV FREYTAG.
25. **The Kiddle-a-wink.** By Mrs. NOTLEY.
26. **Jean Valjean** (Les Misèrables). By VICTOR HUGO
27. **Cosette and Marius** (Les Misérables). By VICTOR HUGO.
28. **Fantine** (Les Misérables). By VICTOR HUGO.
29. **By the King's Command.** By VICTOR HUGO.
30. **The American.** By HENRY JAMES, Junr.
31. **The Conspirators;** or, Cinq-Mars. By A. de VIGNY.
32. **Genevieve,** and **The Stonemason.** By A. LAMARTINE.
33. **Love's Bitterness;** or, The Story of Patience Caerhydon. By Mrs, NOTLEY.
34. **The Brownrigg Papers.** By DOUGLAS JERROLD. Edited by BLANCHARD JERROLD.
35. **The Mistress of Langdale Hall.** By ROSA MACKENZIE KETTLE, Author of "Smugglers and Foresters."
36. **Marriage Bonds.** By C. J. HAMILTON, Author of "Flynns of Flynnville."
37. **Smugglers and Foresters.** By ROSA MACKENZIE KETTLE, Author of "Hillsden on the Moors," &c.
38. **Hillsden on the Moors.** By ROSA MACKENZIE KETTLE.
39. **A Face Illumined.** By E. P. ROE, Author of "From Jest to Earnest," &c.
40. **Under the Grand Old Hills.** By ROSA MACKENZIE KETTLE.
41. **Fabian's Tower.** Ditto
42. **The Wreckers.** Ditto
43 **My Home in the Shires.** Ditto.
44. **The Sea and the Moor.** Ditto.
45. **Holiday House.** By C. SINCLAIR, Author of "Modern Accomplishments," &c.
46. **The Sunny South.** By Captain ARMSTRONG, Author of "Sailor Hero," &c.
47. **The Flynns of Flynnville.** By C. J. HAMILTON, Author of "Marriage Bonds."
48. **No Sign,** and other Tales. By Mrs. CASHEL HOEY, Author of "Blossoming of an Aloe," &c.
49. **The Blossoming of an Aloe.** By Mrs. CASHEL HOEY.
50. **The Mad Willoughbys,** and other Tales. By Mrs. LYNN LINTON.
51. **In the House of a Friend.** By Mrs. NOTLEY, Author of "Love's Bitterness."
52. **Paid in Full.** By HENRY J. BYRON, Author of "Our Boys, &c.

London: WARD, LOCK & Co., Salisbury Square, E.C.

www.ingramcontent.com/pod-product-compliance
Lightning Source LLC
LaVergne TN
LVHW020026170826
845678LV00001B/133
* 9 7 8 0 3 5 3 6 3 7 4 8 1 *